PRAISE FOR *THINKING OUTSIDE THE BOSS*

"Oskhar Pineda is the kind of leader every business needs. He gets it: success isn't just about the bottom line—it's about empowering the people around you to shine."

—MEL ROBBINS, *NEW YORK TIMES* BESTSELLING AUTHOR, HOST OF *THE MEL ROBBINS PODCAST*

"*Thinking Outside the Boss* is a profound reminder that leadership is not about commanding from the top but fostering a culture of trust, vulnerability, and mission-driven teamwork. With decades of success in the construction industry, Pineda demonstrates how prioritizing people over profits creates organizations where employees thrive, productivity soars, and businesses achieve sustainable success. This book is an essential read for anyone looking to redefine leadership and build workplaces where everyone, from employees to customers, benefits."

—DR. MARSHALL GOLDSMITH, THINKERS50 #1 EXECUTIVE COACH, *NEW YORK TIMES* BESTSELLING AUTHOR OF *THE EARNED LIFE*, *TRIGGERS*, AND *WHAT GOT YOU HERE WON'T GET YOU THERE*

"The formula for directing a high-achieving organization is not that difficult even if the steps to implement it can be. Oskhar Pineda simplifies both: build a community where your people are invested in their work and care about each other. Productivity improves, profits rise, and everyone is being the best version of themselves. *Thinking Outside the Boss* is a brilliant reminder to entrepreneurs and other leaders to do everyone a favor and get out of their own way."

—JOSH LINKNER, *NEW YORK TIMES* BESTSELLING AUTHOR, FIVE-TIME TECH ENTREPRENEUR, VENTURE CAPITAL INVESTOR

"Too often, people in charge forget that leading an organization is first and foremost a people game. Take care of your employees, they'll take care of your customers, and your customers will take care of your business. Everybody wins. Oskhar's been grinding for thirty years with phenomenal results and his life is testament to this truth. Read *Thinking Outside the Boss* and become inspired to do the same."

—RYAN ESTIS, AUTHOR, KEYNOTE SPEAKER AND FOUNDING PARTNER, IMPACTELEVEN

"What sets *Thinking Outside the Boss* apart is its authenticity. Oskhar's journey and experiences are woven into every chapter, making his insights not just theoretical but deeply personal and actionable. Oskhar's wisdom, humility, and passion for leadership shine through every page. This book doesn't just teach you to think differently— it challenges you to lead differently. It has left a profound impact on me, and I'm confident it will do the same for you."

—SAM THEVANAYAGAM, PRESIDENT AND CEO AT PARTS LIFE, INC., DEVAL LIFECYCLE SUPPORT, AND LC ENGINEERS, INC.

"Oskhar Pineda has spent decades as the boss, and he knows what many in charge aren't willing to admit: leadership should not be a top-down structure. Organizations don't excel when team members rely on the person at the top to handle the tough stuff that inevitably hits the fan; they excel when leaders mentor, share, and empower. Oskhar is a prime example of radical humility in action, and the principles in this book serve as a guide for leaders at any stage of their careers to embrace."

—URS KOENIG, FORMER UN PEACEKEEPER, FOUNDER OF THE RADICAL HUMILITY LEADERSHIP INSTITUTE, BESTSELLING AUTHOR OF *RADICAL HUMILITY: BE A BADASS LEADER AND A GOOD HUMAN*

THINKING
OUTSIDE
THE BOSS

www.amplifypublishinggroup.com

*Thinking Outside the Boss: The Four Uncommon Leadership
Principles to Equip Your People and Build Your Organization*

For more information, please contact:
Amplify Publishing, an imprint of Amplify Publishing Group
620 Herndon Parkway, Suite 220
Herndon, VA 20170
info@amplifypublishing.com

Library of Congress Control Number: 2024925220

CPSIA Code: PRV0125A

ISBN-13: 978-1-63755-710-5

Printed in the United States

*This book is dedicated to all the employees
that I had the privilege to mentor, guide, and
learn from . . . thank you. You helped me become
a better leader and human being.*

THINKING

OUTSIDE
THE BOSS

**THE FOUR UNCOMMON
LEADERSHIP PRINCIPLES**

to Equip Your People and
Build Your Organization

OSKHAR PINEDA

amplify

an imprint of Amplify Publishing Group

CONTENTS

PREFACE..xi

INTRODUCTION...xv

PART I: VULNERABILITY

Chapter 1: Opening the Door 1

Chapter 2: Vulnerability Is Not Weakness 13

Chapter 3: Leadership in the Open 27

PART II: COMMUNICATION

Chapter 4: Mixed Signals...37

Chapter 5: Listening to Understand.........................51

Chapter 6: Keeping the Conversation Flowing......65

PART III: TRUST

Chapter 7: Taking a Leap 77

Chapter 8: Building Bonds That Last......................93

Chapter 9: Here to Help 113

PART IV: MISSION

Chapter 10: The Importance of Mission 125

Chapter 11: Seeing around the Corner...................143

Chapter 12: Making the Mission Count..................163

Chapter 13: Thinking Outside the Boss.................171

ENDNOTES 175

ACKNOWLEDGMENTS...185

ABOUT THE AUTHOR 187

PREFACE

In the summer of 2021, in the small Miami suburb of Surfside, Florida, the sudden collapse of a twelve-story beachfront condominium shocked the country. Ninety-eight residents were killed in what was later described as the third-deadliest structural engineering failure in US history.

What went wrong? Later analysis pointed to ongoing degradation of the building's concrete structural support, caused by saltwater penetration and corrosion of the concrete's reinforcing steel. It was not an uncommon problem in southern Florida. In this case, the issue was first reported in 2018, and again a month before the collapse. The building had shown all the signs of distress, with engineering reports to back that up, but people were just not listening, especially those who could have averted the collapse. Only afterward did the tragedy unleash massive changes in building inspection practices, which was perhaps the only positive result of an avoidable disaster.

Thankfully, my company wasn't involved, but the lasting shock of the tragic Surfside collapse weighed heavily on us—as it did on everyone involved in the high-rise building repair and rehabilitation industry. We couldn't help asking, what were the real priorities of the building owners, the city inspectors, and all those responsible for public safety? Why were they unable to see beyond outward appearances and their own internal conflicts to recognize the real warning signs? What prevented them from acting to perform the repairs and avert the tragedy?

The real questions go far beyond building construction. The Surfside disaster—and countless, much less dramatic failures—point to deeper, more pervasive flaws in our approach to business, and to the urgent need for change.

But change does not come easily or automatically. We have a primal need to "have all the answers." This is not only a ridiculous concept in today's complex world, it is also self-destructive. Without a healthy measure of openness and vulnerability, we're likely to become entrenched in our beliefs, rejecting information that can save us from imminent peril. We also mistrust others, sometimes with good cause but often just instinctively. This is equally perilous. It only limits our ability to ask questions, stay current, and prosper accordingly.

An inflated image of self and lack of trust contribute to this dysfunction, but there's more to it. In hindsight, the lack of real communication was obvious in the aftermath of the Surfside collapse. But miscommunication is also a universal (and ironic) flaw in our state-of-the-art, information-laden economy. So too is our perennial lack of shared clarity and passion for one's mission. We're adept at *saying* what our mission is, as every inspirational keynote and poster will attest. But we're not always great at knowing and owning that mission personally, turning it into a working reality. Like humility, vulnerability, communication, and trust, connection and passion for our mission must be learned and practiced. It begins with the leadership taking the first step.

Surfside reminded us that we need to think about leadership differently. Being a good leader means unlearning old, instinctive, and often self-destructive habits and practicing new ones that we can use to build a better foundation—for everything. It means more than expecting team members to follow whatever the boss says. In both everyday activities and in crisis moments, if the accepted patterns result in failure, it is a call to get back to the fundamentals and to "think outside the boss."

INTRODUCTION

When you think about it, all inanimate objects can tell stories. We just need to observe and listen. Think about curated museum collections.[1] Or think of a child's favorite things, or the books and knickknacks in your Zoom background. Ordinary and not-so-ordinary objects can speak volumes. Not everyone listens to these stories. We love the sound of our own voice and the stories we tell ourselves. We easily miss voices that are not our own. But if we take the time to listen, then even the most ordinary object—like the most ordinary person—can say something extraordinary.

* * * *

In my business, through the art of careful observation, we listen to buildings. Each one has a story to tell. No matter when or how they were built, they speak in their own vocabulary of architecture, style, aesthetics, and even society itself. Architects and developers have known this for years.[2] If you've ever walked into a cathedral, an iconic sports venue, or even just a pleasant, well-designed home, you can hear or feel *something*—some kind of connection. And quite often, buildings say a lot about the people who live or work there. But most often, they can tell you how they're doing physically. That's where I come in.

Since 1991, I've built a business working hand in hand with structural engineers' and my team's ability to see, hear, and understand the physical state of large commercial and residential buildings. Over 70 percent of our work involves repairing and rehabilitating their structural issues—from replacing a single support column to rehabilitating an entire structure. But we spend the other 30 percent observing and listening for the signs that will ultimately tell us the condition of the structure. A building can look as good as the day it was built, but appearances can be deceiving. We work with structural engineers to assess and explore the building elements, through controlled, destructive examination, to determine what's happening behind the surface. As we assess the building, we look for the symptoms that a casual observer might miss, like rotation, deflection, bulging, sinking—and cracking, of course. Once we know the building well enough, we work with the structural engineer to repair the deficiencies or preemptively address the effects of time and entropy.

In a way, we are akin to doctors tasked with keeping people healthy. We don't design or construct the building, but we're tasked with having the knowledge and expertise required to keep it structurally healthy. As it is with many professions, listening is an essential skill—one of many skills needed to help others thrive.

Repairing and rehabilitating buildings requires much more than engineering and construction expertise. It also requires working well with (and listening to) people. This is a wider circle than just our own team members. Many individuals and groups are involved, each with their own unique cast of characters—some friendlier and more helpful than others. Each has their own voice. At times, understanding what the *building* is saying is the easy part of our work.

In the case of high-rise buildings, the people involved often have conflicting interests, priorities, and attitudes, especially when the residents are also owners, usually represented by an association and its board of directors. Often, a board's vision and goals are at odds with those of individual members. When it comes to their shared building, the most common conflict is, of course, over how to spend their money.

The next layer, as it were, is usually a professional management company, hired by the owners to manage day-to-day affairs. Here too, the most common source of conflict with owners involves money—how to spend finite resources on a seemingly infinite list of conflicting needs.

Conflicts involving money have another often overlooked aspect. In many cases, people's perceptions and priorities come from looking only at the surface of things. A building's lobby, for example, may take top priority for some, since that's the easiest thing to see. It's in our nature as humans to look first at things that are readily apparent, putting off concerns that are less obvious. But it takes extra effort to listen and observe what's beyond the surface.

Over three decades of working in the construction industry has led me to create a brand of leadership that in theory may seem counterintuitive at first glance. In reality, it is foundational to success. In construction-related fields (or in any business or political endeavor for that matter), the traditional leadership qualities are decisiveness, persuasion, confidence, and the willingness to exercise one's authority. Risk-taking and resilience are also included, as are many other qualities of "highly effective people." However, as valuable as these leadership qualities are, I have created and lived by a fundamental, less alpha-oriented model. Such a model is vital to ensuring any organization's longevity and viability. Simply put, we must think outside the traditional boss model. We must put to work those qualities that make us simply more human as leaders.

Many times, learning (or relearning) these principles can come in the form of a crisis.

* * * *

On Christmas Day in 2014, I was taking a break at my cabin in West Virginia. As I often did to decompress and clear my mind, I was chopping wood for the fireplace, dressed in my fatigues with my phone safely tucked away and on mute. I was enjoying a beautiful holiday without worrying about work issues. But my plans for rest and recreation were about to change.

That day, when I paused to take a breath, I pulled out my phone. There were two voicemails and two missed messages from Fernando, my company's operations manager and a long-time friend. It was rare for him to call during a holiday, so I knew it had to be important. The call was anything but routine.

The messages were chilling. A residential condominium building in the area had experienced a three-floor collapse. That same day, Fernando had received an urgent call from Steve, a structural engineer with whom we had done multiple projects in the past. The building's ownership had called Steve to deal with the collapse.

Steve was (and still is) an expert structural engineer. At the time, the building's owners had hired him to perform an exploratory assessment. My company was not yet involved, but our long-standing relationship was the reason we were his first call.

Steve's work was the result of a contentious dispute among the building's owners over whether to spend their limited funds on beautification projects or on structural improvements. One owner had been particularly strident in these debates, and overall progress had been painfully slow. Steve was one of several engineers hired over the years by the building's owners, and his inspection was barely completed when the collapse occurred.

I immediately returned Fernando's call, asking if anyone had been hurt and about the full extent of the damage. He was en route and did not have many details. I then spoke with Steve, who was already at the scene talking with the property manager, the board president, emergency response crews, and the county building inspector. It was chaotic. When Fernando arrived, we surveyed the damage via FaceTime, and the scope of the collapse started to become clearer.

Miraculously, and to everyone's relief, no one was injured. Only the outer wall of the building had collapsed, but the apartments on those floors were deemed unsafe to stay in, and the structural integrity of the building itself was unknown. By tragic coincidence, one of the affected units was owned by someone who was vocally opposed to structural repairs. In the chaos of those initial hours, one thing became crystal clear: a swift, decisive response was the order of the day. Steve introduced me and my company to the county building inspector during one of several FaceTime sessions. He said the priority was to secure the site. Although not yet under contract, I said we would do so, and he proceeded to get an emergency permit while we summoned a crew to secure and stabilize the site.

The next day, I travelled to the scene. From the moment of Fernando's first messages, the response from my team was decisive and fast—the result of many years of practicing lateral communication and mutual trust. While I was en route, we contacted members of our team. Some just needed to know the situation and be on standby, while others joined me at the site.

Once I arrived, the scope of "securing the site" became even more clear. The brick facing of the floors above the collapse was hanging precariously, making it unsafe to work below the upper floors to install new support columns. Fernando had assembled a crew, and so we devised a plan. Two members of the crew rappelled down from the roof to inspect the wall more closely. They discovered that the brick façade had not been properly anchored to the main structure, so they installed anchors to secure the façade above the collapse. While other members of the crew cleared debris and fenced off the area, we stabilized the structure and were ready to proceed.

Over the following days, new challenges emerged. County officials made it clear that repairs were mandatory. But the owners simply did not yet have the funds to pay for the work. They had requested a loan for the cost of the engineer's more detailed repair plan, but now it would have to be for a much larger amount. To make matters worse, the county later insisted that repairs would have to be performed on the opposite side of the building as well, not just the one where the collapse had occurred. Both sides of the building had shown the same signs of deterioration earlier, but before the collapse, no one was listening.

The situation required a very large dose of two principles described in this book—***vulnerability*** and ***trust***. The owners were just at the start of securing a loan to finance the repairs and were now facing much greater expense. I had no guarantee of payment, *only the trust of my team*. And it was this trust, earned over years of working together, that gave me the conviction to take the risk and agree to begin the work.

A TRUST ORIGIN STORY

In construction-related businesses, trust is a limited commodity. All too often, in the rush to win more projects and drive down costs, the well-being and safety of individual employees is not a high priority. They are simply a resource to be utilized as needed in exchange for a paycheck, but nothing more. Experiencing this on a regular basis, most employees do not trust management to treat them as a valued part of the team, much less as people.

My first exposure to this came at a young age, before I had any experience whatsoever in construction. A friend confided in me that his entire forty-two-man construction crew had walked off the job, and he didn't know what to do to bring them back or hire new people. As a successful salesperson, my profession before going into construction, I felt I knew enough about people in general to help with the situation. (Another factor was that most of the crew spoke mostly Spanish, as did I.) So I agreed to help him solve his predicament.

In the first week I spent working with him, it became clear that, in addition to being wildly temperamental, he was exclusively transactional with his employees—a top-down, do-as-I-say-or-else type of boss. It was all about the money—not an uncommon thing in the "greed is good" 1980s. He had pushed the crew to the breaking point—and break away they did.

Over the weeks that followed, I convinced everyone to return, started a series of conversations with them to figure out what they wanted and needed (especially on safety issues), and began to facilitate a better working environment. As their trust in me grew, so did the company's prospects. I was new in this business, so I had to learn it quickly. I spent many late nights cramming, researching, and getting technical literature (Google did not exist then) from technical reps, the library, and vendors. The business part was important, but in my dealings with the crew, I realized that nothing would work if the employees were not engaged in what they did. My mission was to create an environment where they could work safely and have the opportunity to grow. As I started building that environment, productivity took off and their attitude changed. It was the genesis of a mutual trust that has persisted to this day as I write this book. This trust-based relationship produced the financial success of that company and of the business I subsequently founded.

With the site secure, the engineer and my team began the process. He also had no guarantee of payment, but he rapidly developed a mitigation and repair plan, which the county approved. We began the repair process, replacing the collapsed components and strengthening the rest of the building. As we had done on countless other projects, our team exercised its prowess, not only in the physical reconstruction itself but also in implementing the other two principles described in this book—great communication and a clear focus on our mission.

Two months into the project, our efforts were rewarded. The loan had come through. Our lateral communication and trust had also expanded beyond our team. The property management team and the board became trusted allies. Most of all, our collective clarity and passion for the project's mission grew as each piece of the puzzle came together. Even before we received final payment, the project had become a metaphor for "thinking outside the boss." Our practice of vulnerability and trust, combined with agile communication and clarity of mission, had borne good fruit.

Like other projects before and since, this event highlighted the importance of listening to issues rather than being led by optics—the way things only appear to be. In our experience, this level of vulnerability—accompanied by open communication, trust, and clarity of mission—is essential. Leading others with these principles opens the door to creating a successful company.

To me, physical buildings are symbols of a larger reality. Businesses, governments, and other organizations—just like buildings—may start out well planned and constructed. On the outside, they can *seem* sound, but over time, entropy and neglect will take their toll. Like many of the building owners in this case, leaders of a business can get comfortable with the *status quo*— focusing on (and complaining about) matters of appearance but ignoring signs of actual danger until it's too late.

Too often, business leaders focus on the wrong things—such as awarding perks to address the symptoms of an ailing culture, rather than listening for and responding to the underlying reality.

To grow and restore our businesses to full health, we need to deprioritize the *appearance* of well-being and really listen to what our organization is saying to us. To do so is to begin building a different, more sustainable leadership path.

* * * *

Underpinning each of the principles in this book is a character quality long valued by philosophers and spiritual leaders—a quality unfortunately absent in much of the business world: *competent humility*. Competent humility is a mindset of recognizing one's own expertise and wisdom while at the same time acknowledging that our competence is not yet complete. There is always something to learn. We're quick to notice the lack of humility in others, especially those who have failed spectacularly. It's one thing to diagnose pride in easy targets like Bernie Madoff. It's another matter to see it clearly in ourselves. *Competent humility is a learned behavior*, but once we learn it, we'll be able to master the book's principles.

This book is arranged in four parts that represent those very principles—principles that have served me well for many years. You need not follow them in order, but it may prove helpful to do so. Here they are:

Vulnerability—This is the most difficult concept for leaders (and people in general) to grasp in today's highly competitive business climate. Vulnerability is all too often equated with weakness. In Part I, we will debunk this myth. Vulnerability in a business context is a source of great strength. Properly used and expressed, it allows leaders to be open about their limitations while also consciously taking worthwhile risks. Over time, this increases transparency while also building up the trust and communication qualities of each team member.

Communication—Volumes have been written on this topic, but ironically, the basic principles and the *substance* of communication are often lost in the noise of today's business. Part II will deal not only with those basic tools and how to prioritize them but also with the essential qualities of vulnerability and trust that make true lateral communication possible. In an era where everyone is overly connected—all the time and by every possible means—we need to know how true communication works and why it matters. As every smartphone user of social media will tell you (if he is being honest), we can be connected but not really communicating in a meaningful way.

Trust—Traditional business leaders often expect or demand trust from their people, but to receive trust, you must give it first. The leader must be the initiator of this loop. Rigid, chain-of-command organizations have this problem. The larger the hierarchy, the fewer opportunities there are to build mutual trust. For such connections to thrive, organizational structure must be *flatter*—less vertical and more reliant on lateral connections. In Part III, we will explore what that means. Like vulnerability, trust is not a sign of weakness but a great source of strength. Taking a leap, as it were, is not an isolated exercise but a practical, ongoing (perpetual) state of mind in a healthy organization.

Mission—This final piece is the binding element that makes the other three possible. But it also depends on the existence of vulnerability, communication, and trust. Clarity and passion for your organization's mission, or even for an individual project, cannot exist in a vacuum. As stated earlier, they are all interconnected, like the components of a sound physical structure. In Part IV, we'll explore some of the practical aspects of this fourth principle. A mission statement has to be more than a poster or plaque on a wall. It should never be written for the customer or used as a marketing tool. A leader's mission must be employee-based and have meaning and purpose for each individual member.

At the conclusion of each of these four sections, you will find some hypothetical but practical scenarios and questions. I encourage you to put yourself in a "what if" mode and see where and how these principles could apply to you.

* * * *

The book's title *Thinking Outside the Boss* is more than just a play on words. It's a call to truly define how we think of ourselves as leaders. The recent "quiet quitting" phenomenon is only a warning. The old model of leader-as-hero simply doesn't work as it used to (if it ever really did), especially in an era where employees desire greater autonomy and respect. They ask that their leaders admit to being human, and leaders need to act accordingly. They seek a more relatable, trust-based, human-to-human leadership, free of fear, with a clear mission and purpose.

These four principles have vastly magnified my own business success, as well as that of my colleagues and partners—some of whom have gone on to create their own successful ventures. It is my fervent hope that these principles will do the same for you.

PART I

VULNERABILITY

CHAPTER 1
OPENING THE DOOR

The courage to be vulnerable is not about winning or losing, it's about the courage to show up when you can't predict or control the outcome.

—BRENÉ BROWN

From birth, humans are supremely self-centered beings. As infants, we're protected from harm by parents and caregivers. Sometimes this protection may be overdone, but even when practiced in moderation, it serves to reinforce our innate, unconscious needs and wants. In some families and in some cultures, protection takes the form of control and conformity—sometimes pushed to extremes.

In time, we learn reluctantly that we're not the center of the universe, and that we share the world with others. We grapple with the idea, some more successfully than others, that people besides ourselves have needs. We also learn that conformity is a mixed blessing, but that it's often safer to be silent than to say something audacious. As we adapt to the real world, more or less, our cultivated instinct for self-preservation remains strong.

By the time we reach adolescence, we've developed habits that define us as adults. Some are healthy, like a strong sense of self-worth and the ability to set reasonable boundaries. Others are less so. Fear of appearing weak and inadequate or fear of exposure are natural in unfamiliar situations, but these fears also make it hard to admit mistakes or make us afraid to open up. These instincts lead us to dig emotional moats and build protective walls, so to speak, that make us less approachable and less trusting of others.

Without question, this is an inhibiting factor that undermines our ability to lead. Behind these barriers, it's natural to suspect—or at least filter—voices from outside. With all the pressures to succeed amidst strong competition, it is tempting to think and act like the smartest person in the room. We seldom are. The world is too big and moving too fast for any one person to anticipate what happens next—much less to have all the answers. But our inner narrative stubbornly declares otherwise. Like the limbless Black Knight in *Monty Python and the Holy Grail*—or the executives in the "too big to fail" banks in 2007—we refuse to acknowledge our own failings. When we do so continuously, our endeavors are doomed to fail.

When we see this behavior in others, the answer seems obvious, but it's not easy to acknowledge in ourselves. Think of every fall-from-grace story you've ever read, watched, or heard of. Failed politicians, media stars, athletes, and tycoons all share a common thread. They thought they had it all, and their ego was the seed of their downfall. But while you're nodding in agreement, ask yourself if you would have thought or done differently.

We all have individual gifts and talents. They are what make us uniquely human. These talents are valuable in and of themselves, but how often do we admit that they work best when coupled with those of others? Just the thought of admitting that we don't know the answers to every question or situation is hard to fathom. It makes us feel exposed. Deep down, we're afraid that we'll fail or that we'll be diminished in others' eyes. Our walls are there for a reason. Now the question is, how do we open a door in those walls?

The Power of Saying "I Don't Know"

Competitive team sports require secret plays and signals. Team members signal each other hoping their opponents don't know what pitch or play or move is coming next. It's what makes the game exciting. But when that secrecy is misapplied by team leaders who are "stuck in their own heads," the results are disastrous. In the comedy *Bull Durham*, the cocky young pitcher inevitably fails each time he shakes off the signals of his seasoned but cynical catcher. In the real world of sports, there are many less humorous examples of star players and coaches who fail because "their way" was unyielding to adjustment or input from others on their team.

The sport of soccer is probably a more apt metaphor. It illustrates the advantage of vulnerability—and the disadvantage of closing yourself off from others. On the pitch, even the most gifted player is on an equal footing, so to speak, with every other teammate. Give and take is the nature of the game. Coaches on the sidelines do not dictate set plays. The flow of play is continuous, and both captains and players must remain open to new opportunities.

The widely acclaimed series *Ted Lasso* captures this dynamic. The title character epitomizes the truly vulnerable leader. Throughout the series, Lasso is a naïve, folksy American amateur thrust into the leadership of an English Premier League professional football club. "Heck, you could fill two internets with what I don't know about football," Lasso says. As the series progresses, his admitted lack of knowledge conceals a deeper understanding of people and the need to be fearlessly open.

The Lasso character is flawed; his own fears and reticence are revealed throughout the series. But the central aspect of his naïve-seeming leadership style is his humility, his openness, and his persistent vulnerability to others. His seeming incompetence when it comes to football masks a deeper competence in understanding the needs of others. Other characters experience the ripple effects of this, initially resisting but eventually becoming more open and vulnerable themselves. In fact, the two characters who remain closed and invulnerable (a petulant billionaire and a scheming club owner) are the series' only tragic figures.

The show is, after all, merely a pleasant fiction, but the writing serves a deeper purpose. To admit not knowing everything and to show moral humility is a difficult but liberating experience. It also produces results. When leaders do so consistently, one study has shown, their followers are less likely to commit unethical behavior and more likely to help others who are having trouble or those with heavy workloads.[1] An earlier research study also found that when leaders behave humbly, followers emulate their behavior, creating a shared interpersonal team process, focusing on achieving the team's highest potential and ultimately enhancing team performance.[2]

* * * *

Admitting one's challenges is a rare thing in business. A 2017 study by Leadership IQ, surveying over 27,000 executives, managers, and employees, reported that only 35 percent of all respondents said their organization frequently or always shares openly the challenges it faces.[3] The "always" part of that group was only 15 percent. But according to the *Forbes* article, the irony is that "if an employee does believe that their company always openly shares its challenges, they're about ten times more likely to recommend it as a great employer."

Admitting that you don't have all the answers yields incredibly positive benefits. First, it relieves everyone on the team from the burden of unrealistic expectations. Maintaining the pose of an all-knowing expert is exhausting and, in the end, is likely to result in disappointment, disillusionment, and eventual loss of business. Dropping the pretense has the opposite effect, bolstering morale and ultimately generating goodwill outside the team itself.

Second, the benefit to admitting not knowing everything is a sharp rise in curiosity and engagement. When everyone on the team shares this mindset, it's a signal for everybody to work together to find the answer! This builds confidence in the team's ability to go beyond the surface and dig deeper.

The third benefit is an increase in mutual trust, as we will explore in Part II. When leaders stop pretending that they have all the answers, and a make room for team members to fill in the gaps, they are taking a risk, to be sure. But when they do so in the context of what they *do* know, and treat others' contributions with equal respect, the other team members will begin to do the same. They, too, will be willing to be vulnerable. Over time, this becomes more habitual. Team members will know from experience that they can trust each other.

The fourth benefit—and one of the reasons for writing this book—is that being vulnerable creates a colossal competitive advantage for your team. This might seem counterintuitive, but as we will explore in the next chapter, being vulnerable does not mean emotionally oversharing, spreading blame, or admitting defeat. It also does not mean undermining or devaluing your own competence. It *does* mean admitting to your humanity, both by being honest and by proactively seizing the opportunity to do better. Such behavior, which I call competent humility, strengthens your teams internally and impacts how customers see you. As the mantra "I don't know but I will find out" pervades your work, customer loyalty inevitably increases.

The Kryptonite of the Hero Model

To admit that one is vulnerable and not all-knowing requires something not often found in human nature, much less in today's business climate: a willingness to step outside your accustomed comfort zone and recognize *publicly* that you're as human as everybody else. For a long time, well before the employee crisis of 2020 disrupted everything, leaders tended to stagnate, relying on actions that seemed to work in the past. This was especially the case when confident, decisive actions made them look good. After all, it's the traditional way of doing things.

The problem is that the "traditional way" often creates a fanciful synthetic image of the boss as a hero, someone whose extraordinary insights and powers make him uniquely qualified to lead others and respond to any crisis. While that sounds pleasant, especially in the mind of the would-be hero, the image has always had a downside. As business ethicist Yonason Goldson pointed out, "many of us indulge the corrosive reflex of trying to knock heroes off their pedestals by seeking out flaws and defects."[4] He goes on to say that when we are presented with an *image* of heroic character and virtue, we respond in one of two ways. "Ideally, we let ourselves be inspired to set the bar higher for our own conduct," he says. "Alternatively," he continues, "we might feel inadequate in their presence, which motivates us to search out reasons for debasing them. *The latter choice allows us to avoid having loftier expectations for ourselves."*

It would be great if more people viewed heroes as aspirational. But the reality is that under the traditional top-down leadership model, we are more often predisposed to find fault. And, despite their admitted strengths, self-proclaimed hero-leaders give us plenty of reasons to do so. Think of any famous leader in technology, entertainment, finance, or any other high-profile business. Pick one who is often portrayed in iconic terms, as "the next Steve Jobs" for example. Now, think about the team dynamic of working with such a person every day.

Inevitably, some who work for such a hero figure will fall in line, singing the praises of their dear leader. Jobs himself enjoyed such a devoted following in his day. But unfortunately, the hero-boss, one who cannot admit shortcomings or gaps in knowledge, is far more likely to invite disdain and criticism, spoken openly or in secret. These exchanges make leaders even *more* defensive and *less likely* to acknowledge their imperfections. When this behavior becomes the norm, leaders and their teams are unlikely to learn from mistakes, are less likely to support one another, and are increasingly prone to relying on outward appearances.

Corporate Duct Tape

So, what does a team or a company look like under the traditional boss-knows-best model? When employees or team members chafe under the one-sided nature of the relationship, they are much more likely to leave. More recently, they're also likely to follow the "quiet quitting" trend, doing the bare minimum required to keep getting a paycheck.

Obviously, this means lower productivity, less innovation, and a greater likelihood of costly errors. But the traditional responses, threats combined with pay increases and giving out more perks to employees, don't address the real problem. At best, the carrot and stick response only covers it up.

Most of us have seen a car, festooned with duct tape, racing along the highway. Maybe a missing rear window has been replaced with a cardboard square lined with layers of the silvery tape. Or perhaps you can see a bumper, or even a whole side panel, barely hanging on thanks to the handyman's secret weapon. Superficially, the vehicle is OK. The car still functions, but we can tell that something is not quite right The cover-up won't prevent the vehicle's underlying problems from manifesting. Sooner or later, the temporary fix will inevitably unravel.

In so many ways, adding employee perks in the corporate world is just as effective as duct tape. It may keep things from falling apart in the short term, but that only serves to conceal deeper problems. Depending on the type of business, these perks can be quite lavish, like gym memberships or gourmet snack bars. Some can be more ordinary, like insurance or self-directed 401(k) plans. For remote workers, they can be as simple as flexible work hours. But as good as many of these may seem, employee perks only mask deeper issues—an environment where the employee is treated as a cog in a machine.

In 2023, Gartner published an article on the need for shifts in management thinking in response to the post-COVID Great Resignation phenomenon.[5] Many companies, the author points out, are focused on short-term, patchwork fixes, not employees' deeper needs for meaning and purpose. They ignore what most agree are basic truths—that employees are people, not just workers, and that value comes through feelings, not just features. The article pointed out that while 82 percent of employees "say it's important for their organization to see them as a person, not just an employee," only 45 percent of employees "believe their organization actually sees them this way."

This mismatch of priorities is not a new phenomenon. In a 2016 PwC survey, when asked to rank the importance of their top three priorities, employees put "meaning in day-to-day work" at 83 percent, while business leaders put it at only 52 percent.[6] Having a "strong sense of community" also ranked higher for employees, at 56 percent, than for business leaders, at 25 percent.

Clearly, incremental pay increases and employee perks are not a substitute for genuine human connection. Although part of the equation, pay and perks alone cannot make an employee feel that she is being heard, valued, empowered, or given a vested interest in the team's mission. Like rote mission statements on a plaque or poster, they only serve to cover up a deeper problem.

Solving that problem means establishing a common cause with everyone's sense of purpose and self-worth: *the confidence that their opinions and observations are respected.* That doesn't rule out criticism or debate. But it does mean that each member must be respectful and open to changing their minds.

None of this is easy or instinctive. But the process of becoming vulnerable, and not covering up the problem, must start with the leader.

The Conductor and the Coach

For leaders tasked with guiding their teams, vulnerability is challenging, especially at first. You must be willing to let down your guard, admit your imperfections, and open yourself up to unwanted criticism. But the benefits far outweigh the costs. When you own and work on your own deficits, you open the door to endless opportunities to learn new skills. Better still, you discover the value of what others bring to the mix, enhancing the quality of your leadership by adding their talents to yours.

Symphony orchestra conductors have a bad reputation for being the opposite of empathetic and vulnerable. Szell, Toscanini, and others were known as extreme perfectionists, and as temperamental tyrants or bullies. But the reality is more complicated. Think of the leadership challenges a conductor must face. He may have personal expertise with only two or three instruments but must deal with a hundred or so musicians playing close to twenty different instrument types.

In interpreting a piece, the conductor must rely not only on the musicians' individual talents or their willingness to follow directions. He must also rely on their ability to push themselves further and even take risks. Leonard Bernstein, for all his personal struggles, was known for his willingness to reexamine every piece of music during rehearsals. It's unknown whether or not he welcomed his musicians' input, but he would often openly admit he'd been wrong about a composition and would work all the harder to discover a fresh approach.

Perhaps a better model of the potential to be a better leader is that of an athletic coach, as illustrated earlier in the fictional Ted Lasso. There are tyrannical coaches, of course, but the opposite is more likely to produce lasting results. A good coach cannot possibly master all the different skills of his specialized players. He must know enough *about* those skills to help players improve, but his central role is to give them opportunity to practice, try new things, and reinforce what works. Once the game begins, the coach is on the sidelines, as a facilitator, not a dictator.[*]

---

[*] Some may argue that American sports like our version of football contradict this idea, with its practice of plays called from the sidelines. It is true that world football or soccer is more player-directed, but a good American football coach is usually the one who trusts his players' instincts.

Becoming this kind of leader means he must commit to putting in the work. The discomfort of being vulnerable will never completely vanish, just as the aches of a good workout will always be there. But as we'll explore in the next chapter, there are effective ways to develop leadership "muscles" that will win the day.

Vulnerability is a commitment to a way of life, not a once-and-done exercise. Keep in mind that you're human—and because the situations you're involved in are driven by humans, mistakes will still happen. You will still have gaps in your game from time to time, and things might not always go as planned. But there is also a strong possibility that people will appreciate your honesty and be much more likely to trust and work with you over the long haul.

Times are uncertain and more complex than they've ever been. In an increasingly interdependent world, being able to freely share knowledge is the pathway to success in the workplace and beyond.

CHAPTER 2
VULNERABILITY IS NOT WEAKNESS

It may sound paradoxical, but strength comes from vulnerability. You have to ask the question to get the answer, even though asking the question means you didn't know.

—MAJID KAZMI, *THE FIRST DANCER*

What exactly does the word "vulnerable," mean? Used in the context of a business book, the common, literal definition is concerning. The *Oxford English Dictionary* doesn't mince words. Derived from a Latin word meaning "wound," it says vulnerability means "exposed to being attacked or harmed, either physically or emotionally." Webster isn't much kinder; vulnerability means being "capable of being physically or emotionally wounded" or "open to attack or damage."

So, why on earth would a business leader put vulnerability at the top of their list of priorities? The answer only makes sense if you think about relationships that have one key ingredient: *competent humility.* When the partners in a romantic, personal relationship view themselves as capable but imperfect, prone to making mistakes but able to learn from them, then most of us think vulnerability is a healthy thing. When a competent team leader does not elevate his own opinions over everyone else's, and is willing to listen to others, then vulnerability is a source of great strength and connection. And when the experienced head of a company seeks input on a complex matter *genuinely*, without presupposing superior knowledge, then his willingness to be vulnerable is an open invitation for others to do the same. Ultimately, the group and its mission can only benefit.

Here's a heads-up about vulnerability. When a leader admits not knowing the answer to something, there will likely be someone in the group who will respond out of an inordinately high opinion of himself. He may well cause friction or conflict by using that opinion as a cudgel. Be prepared for it. In randomly selected groups of humans, the likelihood of having someone prone to self-focused or narcissistic behavior today is around 6 percent.[1] We are dealing with flawed humanity, which means that being vulnerable involves taking risks, but don't take it personally; keep forging ahead. This is part of putting in the work.

Unchecked, negative human responses make it harder to remain vulnerable and have open-ended discussions. However, the cost of *not* being open is even higher, even if it's not fatal. When a matter being discussed is relatively small, as in a status meeting for a single project, the lack of openness in a leader—or in their colleagues—can seem small. After all, it's easy to accept the *status quo* and not raise questions if the boss "knows what he's doing" and is not open to questions. But in the long run, and when the stakes are high, and when the processes are complex, being "invulnerable" and closed to others' opinions is not only unrealistic. It will eventually lead to disaster.

The *Challenger* Challenge

In the days before the web (only thirty-plus years ago), it was much easier to feign knowledge, both individually and as part of a project. It was also easier to shift or otherwise avoid blame. If the effects were minimal, or impacted only a few people, it likely would never see the light of day. A mistake might have had long-term business effects, but by the time it came to light, those who triggered the problem might have been long gone. Things are different now.

For all its flaws and potential for harm, the web—and social media in particular—have opened every aspect of human activity to unfiltered scrutiny. What was once the sole province of investigative journalists, prosecutors, and congressional committees is now an open book. This has caused many leaders to react defensively, becoming even less vulnerable, taking great pains to conceal their activities, and hiding behind an illusion of all-knowingness—or at least an extreme aversion to saying, "I don't know." But as so many have learned the hard way, the truth of any matter will eventually leak out.

So, instead of pretending to be invulnerable, what would it look like if leaders were not afraid of appearing human, and were willing to ask for answers to their gaps in knowledge? In the age of unavoidable scrutiny, what would it be like if leaders practiced *purposeful* vulnerability?

* * * *

On a cold morning in January 1986, the space shuttle *Challenger* exploded only minutes into its well-publicized launch. Most of us remember exactly where we were and what we were doing when we heard the news. We clung to hope and notions that someone had seen parachutes deploy, or that somehow the crew had survived. They did not. The media of the time—like its accelerated social media successors today—amplified the trauma. As the shock subsided, investigations revealed that the problems were identifiable, but had been ignored.

Months before launch, someone at Morton Thiokol, the company that built the shuttle's twin boosters, knew there was a problem.[2] Roger Boisjoly, a staff engineer, determined that extreme cold would affect the boosters' rubber O-rings, hardening them and making them less flexible. This would allow hot, combustible gasses to escape, creating the very situation that caused the explosion. Later reporting revealed that although an earlier engineers' meeting at the Thiokol factory raised alarms, no one called the NASA administrator or the launch director.[3]

Morton Thiokol was ultimately blamed for the disaster, but Boisjoly was penalized for telling the truth. At the time, and during the investigation, he was shunned and removed from space project assignments. Following trauma-related medical leave, Boisjoly resigned and became a well-respected lecturer on organizational behavior and ethics. He was belatedly recognized for his integrity and courage.

Those involved in the *Challenger* launch did not have all the necessary facts, nor did those in the chain of command have sufficient openness of mind to consider all the warning signs. The agency was under tremendous pressure to launch, in order to prove the program's cost-effectiveness and commercial potential. It was a massive and complex project, almost beyond imagination, but the culture of the time was not one where dissent could be easily heard. The focus at the top was on appearances, notably the public relations buzz of having a civilian school teacher, Christa McAuliffe, on the seven-person crew. Bad weather and technical delays put leaders under even more pressure to launch. But the overriding problem was cultural. Safety was a top concern at NASA—as it is to this day. But in such a vast, hierarchical organization, appearances mattered more than they should have.

In the end, fear of looking bad or appearing weak made it difficult to admit the possibility of being wrong—or not knowing all the answers. Sadly, as is still true today, circumstances and the culture precluded the possibility of being purposefully vulnerable.

* * * *

Hindsight is always 20/20, but the *Challenger* explosion can still serve as a vivid reminder—pointing us to the need for a different approach. Of course the greatest lesson is that ***concealing a defect is never beneficial in the long run***. The principle is the same, even though the phrase "long run" has changed in meaning, thanks to the immediacy of social media. The warning signs for *Challenger* may have been known sooner if it happened today, but if the players retained the same mindset, equating vulnerability with weakness, the bad outcome would still be likely.

The challenge, therefore, is to rethink our role as leaders—and the role of all those we are leading. Vulnerable leaders should not minimize their own competence and importance to the team, but neither should they view their role as all-important. Like a steering wheel on a car, the leader's role is crucial to the group's direction and purpose. But the cotter pins securing the car's critical parts, or the brake pads and a hundred other components, are just as important. Acknowledging others' areas of expertise—even when they eclipse a leader's own knowledge—is the key to every successful launch.

The Dos and Don'ts of Vulnerability

As we touched on in the first chapter, being vulnerable has its benefits. It relieves us from the burden of having to be right all the time—which is an illusion anyway. It also arouses a healthy curiosity among one's team members, in the minds of your customers, and even within yourself. The simple admission that you might not have an answer opens the way for innovative thinking and problem-solving. Not every new idea will be great, of course. But when those around you are also vulnerable, new ideas and solutions have space to breathe.

Most important, vulnerability keeps you fresh and current. It is key to long-term competitive advantage over those who claim to know it all. Customers can usually see through such claims, and are attracted to someone who is genuinely seeking answers. That can only happen when that someone knows there's always something new to learn.

There are right ways and wrong ways to express vulnerability. First, always **admit your humanity, but don't dwell on defeat**. When something goes wrong, a blanket emotional admission of defeat may feel cathartic in the moment, but it will do more harm than good. When you merely throw yourself to the mercy of your teammates or your customers, you're asking *them* to take the reins. You're abdicating the burden of responsibility, which may be a relief to you, but it will only foster resentment. But if you admit to being human **and** take responsibility for making things right, you keep the responsibility where it belongs—with you.

Second, vulnerability must always be **authentic, not synthetic**. This means having an honest inventory of your own potential assets and liabilities. Your expert knowledge and skills are part of the former, but they are not unlimited. You can always learn more. It also includes knowing your and your team's temperamental and emotional capacities. Sometimes working through a problem means navigating through relational issues honestly, not pretending that everyone is feeling great. Keeping such matters confined to emotional silos is a recipe for disaster.

Authenticity also means a commitment to look beyond appearances—not only in each immediate situation but also in your overall relationships with team members and customers. What may look like a solid wall or a firm foundation may contain fatal flaws that only honest, expert exploration can reveal.

A third important distinction is that real, transparent vulnerability is *sincerely solution-focused, not an attempt to emotionally appease or seek forgiveness*. Admission of a mistake only carries weight when you are committed to a long-term solution and the best interests of the customer. Fear of losing business, next to the fear of looking weak or of being penalized, is often the excuse for *not* being transparent, but giving in to those fears will have only negative outcomes. Instead, a truly transparent response is to *be accountable for both sides of the problem*—admitting the mistake while also advocating for a solution that includes everyone's input—a state known as *competent humility*. It means being knowledgeable and decisive, committed to following through, while also being open to thoughts other than your own. These are the marks of real vulnerability.

True vulnerability can never become a license for abusive behavior—of yourself or of others. It requires mutual accountability and trust within the entire team, as we will expand on in Part III. When practiced by all, vulnerability is the key to much greater things. But the first step is to practice these principles in a controlled environment.

Barriers to Change

Even when we acknowledge the wisdom of vulnerability, it's hard to put into practice. It is not necessarily a moral failing. Human nature is loaded with contradictions; we often act against our own best interests—for reasons we only dimly understand. Practicing competent humility and being purposefully and intelligently vulnerable sounds great, but it doesn't come naturally. We often react instinctively (and incorrectly) without a lot of conscious thought.

Noted psychologist Daniel Kahneman sheds light on this dilemma. In his book *Thinking, Fast and Slow*, he explains the two human systems that drive the way we think and act.[4] What he calls System 1 is that part of us that operates automatically and rapidly, with little effort or sense of voluntary control. It's what happens when we drive a familiar route to the grocery store but have no idea of what happened along the way. System 2, on the other hand, allocates our attention to effortful mental activities, including complex calculations, that the situation demands. The problem, he explains, is that we naturally prefer to spend less effort when we can. The System 1 response is usually easier, but it can be wrong.

It is these unconscious cognitive biases that lead us into over-confidence. We naturally tend to simplify and generalize, even when the actual situation is quite complex, and imagine that our own knowledge is sufficient to handle it without outside help. Of course when we stop to think about it (System 2), we realize that we need others' input, but it's cognitively easier to "go with our gut." And if our fears of being exposed or blamed are reinforced by our business culture, then it is that much easier to keep our doubts and questions to ourselves.

Another common barrier is closely related to our personal cognitive biases. As a group or team, we often focus on the immediate, short-term goals of a particular project. It's relatively easy to set these and understand them, but there is a downside. For example, formal key performance indicators (KPIs) are important tools to measure progress toward business goals. They can also ensure that everyone is aligned with those goals, and that performance can be judged more objectively. But KPIs structured around short-term goals sometimes impair our ability to envision long-term ones. In some cases, they can even stifle creativity and innovation.[5]

This isn't an indictment of KPIs or performance measurement. Businesses today need every possible way to improve their performance and eliminate waste. However, such methods can make it harder for a leader to recognize input or warning signs that were not baked into the original calculations. Technology platform developers, for example, have become frighteningly efficient at measuring human responses to their algorithms, and fine-tuning them for their own profit. But at the same time, they have remained oblivious to the larger social issues of creating what some have called "weapons of mass distraction."

A third barrier to purposeful vulnerability is not psychological, social, or narrowly economic, but is in fact related to old-fashioned morality—or rather the lack of it. By nature or upbringing (probably both), all too many of us are driven by fear, greed, and an inflated ego, something once known as pride. Being self-protective, desiring more of a good thing, or thinking we're oh, so very special may be natural, but they are not our noblest impulses.

The decision to be vulnerable is not always cognitively easy—or aligned with our short-term business goals. It's also a decision we often ignore if it conflicts with our own selfish nature. So how do we change our ways? If it's true that ethics and morality are defined as what you do when no one is looking, then we need to consider two things. First, everyone *is* looking. We're living in the social media–fueled era of "living in the public eye." Even if we could hide the consequences of our actions for a time, that time is shorter than ever. Sooner or later (more likely sooner), someone will find out you're no superhero. Second, being willing to admit you don't know everything has its advantages—often profound ones.

The Safety Harness Method

Exercising these "muscles" doesn't happen overnight. Our cognitive habits and flaws invariably get in the way. In my years in business, I've found the best way to practice vulnerability is to start in controlled environments involving your immediate team. Other parts of your organization, your partners, and your customers will catch on in time, but the changes that matter always start at the leadership level—with you.

The US Coast Guard goes to great lengths to prepare its people to cope with challenging situations. Seeing a televised helicopter rescue of civilians from boats or flooded homes is dramatic, but what you don't see is more important. Guardsmen spend countless hours practicing with rescue baskets, safety harnesses, and other gear before they go on actual missions. At all times, both the rescuer and the person being rescued are vulnerable and uncertain of success, but the former is better prepared to perform.

The safety harness is an apt metaphor for developing mutual vulnerability and trust, which we will also cover in chapter 8. Like the Coast Guard, my own company used them—along with an array of cables, counterweights, motors, safety devices, and lifelines—to keep our people safe when working to repair buildings. But the *way* we prepared ourselves to use this gear is an exercise in vulnerability itself.

Twice a year, we conducted a company-wide all-hands-on-deck interactive safety meeting. There were a few lecture-style sessions, but the bulk of the time was spent listening and doing—setting up and becoming more familiar with the gear we depended on. Each team member could ask questions, even when the root of a question was a personal concern for life and limb. Most of us were good with heights; it went with the job. But no concern was discounted or minimized. It was an opportunity for the leaders to practice listening, and help everyone get comfortable asking questions without fear of repercussions.

Every Monday, we also held "toolbox talks," where the discussions revolved around upcoming practical issues relevant to specific projects, including safety concerns, or maybe even current news or events that may impact the work. As with the safety meetings, every member was free to offer their input and ask questions without fear of repercussions. This was an excellent opportunity for leadership to walk the walk, by constantly practicing what we preached about openness and vulnerability.

In essence, these events were controlled real-time training exercises with a serious purpose outside a "lab-like environment." When people began working in my company, many were hesitant to speak their minds. Sometimes it's cultural, as when an employee is used to an authoritative family or political system. Often, it's just the product of habitual self-preservation or fear of being ridiculed or penalized. But when exposed to trust and vulnerability in a controlled environment, they begin to respond in kind in their work out in the world.

To foster this dynamic, and to counter our natural instincts for self-preservation, always look for ways to practice as a team, and practice repeatedly, before playing in the "big game."

Transactional or Foundational?

Throughout this book, you will be reading about principles and techniques that may run counter to conventional MBA wisdom. To be sure, there are many valuable, technical processes that every business should consider using. Many of these can even be learned without the benefit of a formal (and expensive) MBA degree.[6] But the availability of all these formulas and methodologies does not address the fundamental issues of leadership. The fact is, *if you understand the **techniques** of modern business, then you are only a corporate technician, but if you truly understand **people**, then you are a leader.*

Practicing vulnerability—first in small, relatively safe groups of colleagues, leading to a broader, more open daily practice—will inevitably change the nature of your business itself, almost as much as it will change and enrich you personally. Vulnerability is the first step away from being a ***transactional*** "I'm only here for the paycheck" business model, which has taken enormous hits in recent years. It is a step toward becoming a ***foundational*** business, one that operates on human values that, coincidentally, make it more successful.

> **IF YOU UNDERSTAND MODERN BUSINESS TECHNIQUES, THEN YOU'RE A CORPORATE TECHNICIAN. IF YOU TRULY UNDERSTAND PEOPLE, THEN YOU'RE A LEADER.**

I sometimes ask how much time in a day my people spend outside their homes. The answer, including long commutes, a full shift at the building site, and well-earned breaks, is around fourteen hours. So, allowing for a reasonable night's sleep, they have only two or three hours for themselves and their families—which is why weekends are sacrosanct. So it only makes sense that people should feel *connected* in a substantial way to those with whom they spend most of their waking hours.

Being vulnerable with one another, and practicing the other "outside the boss" steps described later in the book, is the only alternative to a cold, transactional existence. It's a foundation not only for a successful business but also for a better way of life.

CHAPTER 3

LEADERSHIP IN THE OPEN

I will never have greater respect than for the man that realizes that he was wrong and graciously admits it without a single excuse.

—DAN PEARCE, *SINGLE DAD LAUGHING*

By definition, if you are truly humble and open to admitting your own limitations, you're not likely to be measuring or talking about your own level of vulnerability. Family members or those close to you in business may have their own opinions, but their willingness to tell you where you fall on the "vulnerability scale" is directly proportional to how vulnerable you actually are!

One purpose of this chapter is to give you a chance at self-evaluation. There is no scoring possible. Vulnerability is something revealed by your actions over time, not by a formal exam. Nevertheless, it will help to ask questions of yourself and think about your answers.

QUESTIONS ABOUT VULNERABILITY

Having read the first two chapters, ask yourself the questions that follow, and consider how you might have answered them ten or twenty years ago. Then ask yourself how you might answer them today—or years from now:

- When I ask people on my team if they have any questions, how often do I receive answers that I did not expect?

- When someone on my team makes a suggestion or questions my action, what is my immediate response?

- When it comes to my own professional knowledge and experience, does my opinion match that of my team members?

- How often do I ask team members to help me understand something better, or to contribute new ideas to solve a problem?

- How often do I "let down my guard" when talking with a team member? How often does he do the same?

As I said, there is no score to record here, and if you were expecting to get one, then you probably have a long way to go. The point of the exercise is to help you get to know yourself better.

Now it's time for some role-playing in your imagination. This concluding chapter for Part I is not exactly a workbook, although you're free to use it as such. After considering the self-evaluation questions above, its purpose is to help you step back and look at two purely hypothetical examples and see how you might practice vulnerability in lieu of a conventional, follow-the-boss, do-as-I-say approach. I've already given you the example of my own businesses, so let's look at other industries for inspiration.

High-Tech, High-Stakes

For decades, computer technology has captured the public imagination, and the investment community. From obscure beginnings, digital has become a cultural given, although it feels like the exclusive domain of a few mysterious wizards who control it.

Today's tech obsession is of course artificial intelligence or AI. Once the domain of scary science fiction, AI is at the unrealistic peak of the Gartner "hype cycle."[1] Ordinarily thoughtful, sober analysts, investors, and journalists have imbued it with near-magical possibilities. As reality sets in, disillusionment will become a common refrain, to be followed eventually by normalization of the technology. But for those caught up in the current trend, practicing competent humility (much less vulnerability) is sure to be a challenge.

Our hypothetical company is one of many new AI startups, headed by you, a seasoned tech entrepreneur. You are wise enough to recognize the hyperbole surrounding AI, and have narrowed the company's focus to a single task: medical monitoring. With the right expert understanding of human physiology, the

AI process to more efficiently identify cardiovascular anomalies from routine test results is relatively straightforward.

A typical AI business of this type must have teams of people with particular skill sets. These include a knowledgeable high-level person who can establish the overall data strategy, and someone who serves as a general project manager. There must also be engineers versed in data science, AI, and machine learning, as well as analysts, researchers, and at least the services of an advanced data scientist. Once the project is well underway, the company will also need the services of ordinary business and marketing experts to promote and sell the new technology—not to mention supporting those who use it.

With so much varied, highly specialized expertise, the need for openness and vulnerability is high—and difficult to achieve. In the tech world, it is literally impossible for a leader—or any one individual—to know it all.

There is also the problem of the technology itself. Today's AI-based systems pose a considerable legal, regulatory, and financial risk. If the training data are flawed or biased, or if the AI methodology is poorly executed, companies using it may be exposed to costly repercussions and damage.

AI in medical imaging is also relatively new and prone to embarrassing errors.[2] Add to that the well-established rules for protecting patients' private medical information, which imposes further requirements on data usage.

So, given all these factors, put yourself in the shoes of this hypothetical company's CEO—if you dare. As a leader, how would *you* handle issues of vulnerability?

- As CEO, how should you and your team disclose gaps in your knowledge—to members of the various AI teams, to the company as a whole, and to outside partners or stakeholders? To what extent (and to whom) should you admit mistakes and seek out solutions to unexpected problems?

· As with all technology, experimental failure in AI projects is common. How should you and all other team leaders treat such failures and encourage others to express concern over data quality, bias, or methodology?

· Given the immense time pressures in AI development, how can the team practice vulnerability in a private "safety harness" environment—to be better prepared to do so at work?

· In general, how can team members feel freer to express their opinions without fear of retribution? What can you do to model a safe, open work environment?

There is no question that AI will forever change the way we work. The real question is how can you, as the leader of this hypothetical AI company, embrace vulnerability as part of your leadership strategy? How can you use vulnerability to retain team members and customers, develop a world-class product, and ensure the company's long-term financial success?

Mad Men Revisited

For years, advertising, marketing, and public relations agencies have been criticized—with or without cause—for being more focused on their own revenue than on serving their clients' best interests. Sometimes, they're viewed as lacking in transparency and accountability. Most often, they are criticized when positive metrics, like good Nielsen ratings for TV audiences or high click-through rates for web campaigns, are not accompanied by increased sales.

It's a tricky profession at best. As with many other consultative services, agencies offer a subjective and hard-to-measure result: changes in personal opinion or preference. Ideally, such a change results in more people buying a particular product or service. But it's not an exact science. As retail entrepreneur John Wanamaker famously said, "Half my advertising spend is wasted; the trouble is, I don't know which half."

In such a field, with ad technology changing every five minutes, real expertise counts more now than ever. Recent research suggests that Wanamaker's 50 percent figure was too optimistic.[3] A 2006 study put the overall effectiveness rate of marketing spending at only 37 percent![4] Unlike my business, where literal foundational cracks can be objectively detected and evaluated, seeing cracks in a digital advertising campaign is a challenge— even to industry experts.

What that means is that agency team members—from the CEO to all the account reps, designers, and production specialists—must be at the top of their game. An agency's reputation for practical knowledge is its lifeblood. That makes it tempting to claim greater expertise than one actually has, and to shy away from admitting to any knowledge gaps.

For this exercise, our hypothetical example is a medium-sized digital marketing agency. It was founded by an industry veteran with the sense to hire a diverse team of data experts, designers, and creative talent—along with account reps tasked with really understanding their clients' motivations and needs.

Knowing how important it is to gain a client's trust in a complex digital field, put yourself in the shoes of this agency's president, or any of his team leaders, and ask yourself these questions:

- The subject of AI and marketing will inevitably come up when planning a campaign with your client. How much (and to whom) should you disclose gaps in your knowledge about AI-generated content and its real-world effectiveness in campaigns? How should you disclose any knowledge gaps in related technology, such as SEO or marketing automation?

- You have reasonably good taste in design, but your lead designer has strong opinions—as does the client—when it comes to colors, fonts, or images. How do you handle creative differences over style, without jeopardizing other factors in a campaign?

- It's easy to overlook details when planning a complex marketing campaign. How can you best use others' skills and experience to catch such problems early on, or fix them before they become a major issue?

- Sometimes, campaigns simply fail to fully achieve their goals. It may be due to technical issues or a change in the market, but often it's due to something the team did not plan for. When that happens, what do you tell your team? More important, what do you say to the client? If you take responsibility, what comes next?

- Given the vast complexity of digital marketing, how can your team practice being open and vulnerable, especially with a new or untried process, in a lower-risk "safety harness" environment—before doing so on a larger scale?

- In general, as with **any** business, what can you do to let your team members express their opinions without fear of retribution? What can you do to model a safe, open work environment?

Agencies are, by definition, in the reputation business, so they must be extremely careful when it comes to their own credibility. It is tempting to claim expertise in the latest Adtech method—or in AI—but the chances of being unmasked are extremely high.

The far better approach is to be genuinely vulnerable, both with your teammates and with your clients. As is the case in any business, advertisers and marketers who take responsibility, admit the truth, remain curious, and work harder than ever in the clients' best interests have all the ingredients for their agency's ultimate success.

PART II

COMMUNICATION

CHAPTER 4

MIXED SIGNALS

The single biggest problem in communication
is the illusion that it has taken place.

—GEORGE BERNARD SHAW

No one in business or government will deny publicly the intrinsic value of good communication. Survey after survey proves that both employees and managers *believe* that effective communication has an overwhelming performance benefit, has a direct impact on efficiency, and is essential to developing trust between teams and the organization. But even among entities and individuals who espouse the virtues of good communication, there are many who are shockingly bad at it.

History has many examples of tragic miscommunication. In 1912, had Captain Edward Smith received detailed ice warnings from two other vessels in the vicinity, then over 1,500 people would not have died—and James Cameron would have had to direct a different epic movie.

The problem often lies with human nature. We are all prone to put a good face on a bad situation, especially if pride and hubris are involved. The problem is that the truth eventually leaks out, especially in this age of smartphone cameras and social media. Communicating the actual situation always seems more difficult, but not doing so is worse in the long run.

> ## GOOD COMMUNICATION ALWAYS YIELDS DIVIDENDS; POOR COMMUNICATION COMES WITH SEVERE FINANCIAL PENALTIES.

As we will see later in the book, good communications always yields dividends, both personal and financial. But as too few leaders realize, poor communication comes with severe financial penalties. Before we explore the positive side of effective communication, it is important to understand the economic losses, as well as the negative impact on reputation, incurred by businesses whose members fail to communicate well—or at all. Sometimes, such losses are tolerated or ignored—attributed to "business as usual"—but they always have enormous long-term consequences.

The Nokia Syndrome

Not without irony, one of the most spectacular communication failures in recent years is that of the communications giant, Nokia. The Helsinki, Finland-based tech darling of the 1990s had dominated the mobile and smartphone market, with an almost 50 percent market share of the latter as recently as 2007. The brand's popularity was widely advertised with images of fans holding their mobiles aloft at rock concerts. But today, in the lucrative smartphone market now dominated by Apple, Samsung, and a fleet of other manufacturers, Nokia's market share is only about 3 percent.[1]

What happened? Nokia was *the* major power in a market begun by Motorola's DynaTAC "brick" phone in the early 1980s. They had successfully slimmed down such devices, making them truly mobile. They had also pioneered or advanced important new telecom technologies, such as mobile email, phone web browsers, predictive text, and near-field communication or NFC.[2] Today, Nokia is still a telecommunications player—just ***not*** when it comes to smartphones.

The fundamental problem was a profound absence of communication. The company's brand was sky-high, as were the egos of its executive leadership. While understandably nervous about Apple's mobile aspirations, they created a dictatorial culture—one that discouraged employee feedback.[3] In such a rigid, vertical authority structure, it was unthinkable to question the knowledge and reputation of those higher up—those who had made Nokia number one. In fact, the company possessed much of the technology that would have made it competitive with Apple and others. However, those lower down in the hierarchy were not given the chance to examine that siloed knowledge, much less question or improve it.

The company's lack of internal communication also affected Nokia's external communications. They were slow to perceive changes in consumer trends and equally slow in communicating their products' value. Frequent, sometimes radical changes in hardware and operating system software were not effectively communicated to existing and prospective customers, which led to a frustrating and inconsistent user experience.[*]

In the early 1970s, scholar E. D. Huseman theorized that the

---

*Nokia's strategic indecision is illustrated by confusing, poorly communicated succession of smartphone operating systems. In 2014, they began using, belatedly, a version of Google's Android operating system, joining a large group of OEMs, including Samsung. But before that, the company tried several others, including Symbian (now defunct), the proprietary MeeGo OS, and Windows Phone, which is no longer supported. Since 2021, after selling the phone division to Microsoft and then buying it back, Nokia is now considering dropping Android for an in-house OS. The chaos continues.

cause of Nokia's downfall could be compared to barriers, known as thermoclines, that can occur within large bodies of water, blocking the flow of oxygen and killing aquatic organisms. Organizational communication, he noted, can become stratified, creating barriers based on fear, information hoarding, and misalignment of company goals.[4] Instead of working to eliminate middle managers' fear of sharing "bad" information—by being transparent about their own information and goals—they instead allowed the other fish to starve, so to speak.

Of course, Nokia is not the only company or organization to falter because of poor communication. For all its success in console gaming and entertainment content, the Sony Corporation was singularly unsuccessful in dominating the portable music player market—something they had mastered since the early 1980s. The institutional and technical knowledge that came with the Walkman brand, from cassette players to CDs and MiniDiscs, simply was not communicated well when it came to MP3 players. It wasn't until 2005 that Sony released a viable product, well after Apple had established the iPod (and its captive online music marketplace) as the *de facto* standard.

Communication failures can also have global implications. Energy giants Exxon and BP were infamous for this during the Exxon Valdez and Deepwater Horizon disasters, respectively. Both were criticized for their slow and ineffective response, and for failing to provide accurate information in the early days of each crisis.[5] The Deepwater Horizon event was particularly egregious, as a number of technological issues and test results were not shared between BP and its partners, Halliburton and Transocean.[6]

Communication failures don't have to make headlines to be a serious business problem, however. When a leader or company spokesperson comes across as vague, overuses jargon, is "tone deaf" to the needs of others, or is prone to assigning blame or avoiding transparency, then their so-called communication is perceived as pure BS. An employee may not have the wherewithal to know exactly *why* it stinks, but they can smell it instantly.

Fear-Free Communication

Once, during an inspection of the building at a major retailer (who must remain anonymous), I observed a communications "crack" that was far more serious than the physical one I was there to assess. Everyone I encountered, from the assistant manager to the clerks at their posts, was rigidly focused on only the task before them. They reacted in a profoundly unhappy and terse manner whenever I asked the most casual question. Eventually, I got a straight answer about the physical issue with the building, but the cause of their rigid fear took longer to understand.

As is too often the case, everyone at the firm was under heavy pressure to perform, but they were largely kept in the dark when it came to company goals and aspirations. They were ostensibly on a system of rewards and demerits for how well or how poorly they performed their jobs. The tragedy I discovered was that while demerits were handed down with predictable frequency, rewards simply did not happen—at least for those I spoke with.

This Dickensian situation haunted me long after my visit to that building. How sad that what the company considered communication with its people was decidedly one-way—and overwhelmingly negative. Constructive feedback, if there had ever been any, had been quashed. Fear was the underlying ethos; everyone's day was reduced to a base, transactional level. Those who remained were there solely for the paycheck, and would do or say nothing to further the company's interests. I doubted, as I do to this day, that this company could ever thrive without the input and ideas of those they employed.

* * * *

This need not be the case, of course. As we will see, *fear-free communication* is vital to the health of any organization. It involves the free flow of information from and through every person, without the threats or constraints that would render it impersonal and transactional. Each person, no matter what their title is or their level of schooling implies, has the freedom to express and to be heard. They may not always be correct in their perceptions, but if they are consistently denied the opportunity to express them (or are punished for doing so), then they will shut down. It may take more than one such experience, but eventually they'll retreat into transactional mode, putting in what's required (or what they can get away with), collecting the paycheck, and keeping any good ideas to themselves.

The leader of a team must be doubly aware of this dynamic. As the next chapter will show, he must always be on guard against reacting to others' actions out of anger or personal affront. A leader must remember that he is not the source of every good idea; he is the switch that facilitates the flow of ideas.

Think of it as an electric circuit of sorts. The source of its power is not the switch but the battery or generator that derives its energy, ultimately, from the sun. Likewise, the switch does not create the light or mechanical motion or other useful activity. Each part of the circuit has an essential role, including the circuit breaker or fuse that prevents a dangerous overload.

The switch is merely the means of starting the flow of energy to perform a task, just as a good leader is the one who starts the free flow of ideas. The person whose job it is to throw the switch should also be someone who knows and listens to each part of the circuit. Good communication, to complete the metaphor, is the flow of informational "current" by everyone—with confidence in those connected to other steps in the process and without fear that they will be disparaged or ignored.

Theory and Practice

As noted at the beginning of this chapter, a vast majority of professionals *believe* that good communication is essential to a successful business. They also believe that ineffective communication is a root cause of business failures. Here are a few commonly cited statements to this effect:

- Companies with high effectiveness in change management and communication are three and a half times more likely to significantly outperform their peers.[7]

- Well-connected teams are 20 to 25 percent more productive than those who are not.[8]

- Companies that communicate effectively had a 47 percent higher return to shareholders over a five-year period.[9]

- Eighty-six percent of employees believe that ineffective communication is the main reason for workplace failures.[10]

The truth of these statements is not in doubt; for most

business professionals, they are self-evident. But even when the research and survey data are valid, the numbers only show how important good communication is, and how we feel about it. The numbers alone do not show us how to go about creating transparent, equitable connections within a team.

By the Book / Special Delivery

Thankfully, there are examples of companies that *do* practice forms of fear-free communication. From these, we can learn much about how to achieve it. As we explored in Part I, it begins with a leader's vulnerability—a willingness to admit he doesn't know everything and be truly open to others' insights. Such communication is also the foundation for increased trust and adherence to the overall mission. As shown by these two examples, a bookstore chain and a shipping and logistics company, the process can lead to business success, even in uncertain times.

* * * *

Before the invention of film, radio, and television, books were *the* source of knowledge and inspiration throughout the civilized world. But as other media arose, and especially today as the internet and our mobile devices fill every nook of our waking minds, our time and interest in books has declined. The economic victims of this shift are the book publishers and, of course, booksellers.

The past two decades have seen the decline or outright demise of major bookstore chains, including Borders, Waldenbooks, and Crown Books. By one 2011 estimate, the US had 1,100 fewer bookstores than it did twenty years earlier.[11] Similar declines and consolidations have affected independent bookstores, as readers gravitate toward downloadable e-books and audiobooks, and especially as they increasingly order physical books from Amazon and other virtual stores.

One notable exception to this trend is Barnes & Noble. The saga of the century-old chain's successful struggle with Amazon is well documented.[12] It has adapted well to technological change, and has developed strong communication channels with its customers, both in-store and online. In addition, the company has taken an atypically humble stance when it comes to knowing exactly how readers' habits will evolve.[13]

The company's candor about the future has undoubtedly affected its open communications strategy *within* the organization. Among it's over 20,000 employees, the company prioritizes frequent interactive check-in sessions. Before their shifts begin, employees and managers can openly discuss topics related to their targets and individual goals.

The unexpected resilience of physical bookstores has a lot to do with shoppers' ability to explore and discover new titles at their own leisurely pace—something that e-commerce algorithms can only clumsily simulate. An important part of this process is the presence of staff members who are knowledgeable, responsive human beings. By fostering an inquisitive, sharing ethos among its employees, Barnes & Noble has created that personal dynamic, and turned it into a competitive advantage.

* * * *

Another company with an atypical approach to communication is the American-founded, Germany-headquartered shipping company DHL. Started in 1969, it is now the world's largest logistics company, with over half a million employees in over 220 countries and territories, and with plans to eventually make deliveries to the moon.

The company's success is due in part to its comprehensive open-door policy for its many employees. Among other tools, such as opinion surveys and feedback boxes, DHL uses a company-wide mobile app to keep its various teams connected and informed in various areas of the business. In order to close the gaps between team leaders and frontline team members, this facilitates direct employee-leadership communication, creates a clear understanding of workloads and responsibilities, and prioritizes employee feedback to make improvements to support the company's overall mission.

This communication strategy also translates to better connection with DHL's customers, including prompt updates, delivery information, and other details that, taken together, have served to build trust and confidence in the brand. While other delivery services have also taken advantage of such technology, DHL has taken open and transparent communication to a higher level.

Keeping the Door Open

As we'll explore in the next chapter, a vertical, hierarchical authority structure is the bane of truly open communication. Executives and team leaders who have "clawed their way to the top," as it were, are likely to have an inflated view of themselves and their capabilities. They are likely to feel threatened if a lowly employee, or even a slightly less elevated manager or junior executive, were to ever venture their own opinion on something. In that climate, the notion of vulnerability covered in Part I is a foreign concept, and likely to be seen as a threat. So the very idea of having open-door communication is usually dismissed out of hand.

Worse still, in such an environment, bosses may say "my door is always open" in response to social pressure or the words of some management guru. But the reality is that an open door is the last thing they really want. Even the least educated employee in the world can tell that such a declaration is a false promise. And once that promise has been broken, it is painfully difficult to win back an employee's trust.

A vertical authority structure is best suited to foster a ***transactional*** work environment. The boss says such-and-such, and the employees say OK (or nothing), perform the task, and get a paycheck. Instead of addressing human needs such as safety, belonging, and self-esteem, we're left with the pure carrot-and-stick (mostly stick) approach that leaves people shell-shocked and uninspired.

Good communication is predicated on a leader's vulnerability—their admission that they're not the sole source of wisdom and knowledge. They are willing to take everyone's input seriously, despite the emotional bumps and bruises that openness involves, as we'll see in the next chapter. Once practiced consistently, open communication also engenders trust and mutual connection to the team's mission. But a good leader must know that it does not happen overnight.

Open-door leadership promotes the growth of the people we lead, increasing the leader's own success by channeling the creativity and engagement of others—potentially turning them into leaders themselves. But it can only happen when the leader changes the employer-employee relationship *from transactional to foundational.* Employees should get a paycheck, of course, but the essence of the relationship cannot be just about the paycheck—or even the perks. To do this, you must begin to study and apply the four skills detailed in the next chapter. In brief, they are as follows:

- **Know your employees.** They *are* your team. Discover their aspirations and strengths, their goals and motivations. Learn who they are as human beings.

- **Match talent with opportunities.** Look for ways to advance an individual's professional growth. Always be on the lookout for people who show an aptitude for a particular skill—even if it's unrelated to their current task.

- **Envision the results.** Once you have assigned an opportunity, to an individual or the team, do some "future-casting" of the potential benefits.

- **Provide ongoing support.** Stay involved in these opportunities, offering support, helping with roadblocks, and generally providing encouragement.

If this sounds easy, I guarantee it is not. Earlier, I likened the leadership role to that of a switch in an electric circuit. The decision to make that connection—to let the "current" of ideas and action flow through every node of the circuit—is a simple metaphor to imagine in theory. It's also a difficult one to practice in the real world. It takes deliberate practice and patience with your own flaws and those of others, but in the long run, it's worth every ounce of energy you invest in it. The more you cultivate these principles, the more you find opportunities to open doors and create success for others.

It's all about the *quality* of our leadership—not the mechanics—to always be "leading outside the boss."

The evidence of all good business is customer satisfaction—the fulfillment of a basic human need. When that happens, people are motivated and determined to stay with you, and are enthusiastic about saying so to others. But to achieve that goal, our employees must also be happy and motivated by a genuine, shared passion for their work. This happens when we keep the door open, giving them a voice in their own destiny. Productivity will always follow, and customer satisfaction will go from average to awesome.

CHAPTER 5
LISTENING TO UNDERSTAND

*Communication is truth; communication
is happiness. To share is our duty; to go down
boldly and bring to light those hidden thoughts
which are the most diseased; to conceal nothing;
to pretend nothing; if we are ignorant to say so;
if we love our friends to let them know it.*

—VIRGINIA WOOLF, *THE COMMON READER*

Two seminal events in my life prepared me to talk about and practice open communication the way I do. One was unusual, perhaps, but it was simple and relatively straightforward. The other was extremely difficult at first, but over time it proved itself a hundredfold.

When I was in my teens, I was fortunate enough to attend a school that encouraged students to think for themselves. In the school's foyer by the main entrance, there was a blackboard bearing the title "***Vox Populi.***" It's the first part of the old Latin proverb "*Vox Populi, Vox Dei*" or "the voice of the people [is] the voice of God." The blackboard was there for any of us to express anything we wanted to, without fear of repercussions. Only profanity was not permitted.

Needless to say, being full of opinions from an early age, I logged many frequent-flier miles on that board. My comments led to many great conversations with my teachers that I remember to this day. I loved that board; it gave me the chance to be myself, and to be truly free.

The other event centered around my becoming a father. My two daughters were (and are) a constant joy and challenge combined, as all parents know so well. But when each of them was old enough to understand, I made them a solemn promise: no matter what they told me, I said, I would never react in a negative way. I only asked that they tell the truth.

This promise took a few times to sink in, but I stuck to my word, and they believed me. Of course, I was tested in my resolve. Much later, when one of my daughters did something irresponsible, I was disappointed. But I reminded us both of my promise. The consequences of her action were unavoidable, but I assured her I would not react negatively, and asked her to just tell the truth—which she did.

From these events, I learned two immutable truths. First, speaking one's mind honestly, with respect for all, is always a good thing, for everyone. Second, when a leader puts her reactions aside, refusing to respond in a negative manner, then even an uncomfortable truth will not be hidden or suppressed.

Completing the Circuit

In the previous chapter, we likened good communication to an electrical circuit. In our analogy, we compared the leader to the switch that allows the signals (current) to flow freely. But the analogy can do more to help us understand the nature of effective team communication.

Let's start with the easy part—the battery or generator that powers the whole thing. In any team activity, there must always be a source of guidance, inspiration or motivation that powers our activity. In a *transactional* business environment, as we've discussed earlier, the sole source of that power is the promise of a paycheck and/or the threat of losing it. It's a poor bargain at best. The old carrot-and-stick approach, or *extrinsic* motivation, is counterproductive in many if not most situations today. In his 2009 book *Drive*, Daniel Pink noted that "rewards can perform a weird sort of behavioral alchemy." He wrote that they can "transform an interesting task into a drudge" and that they "can turn play into work."[1] This was borne out during and since the pandemic, when many employees realized the futility of their routine jobs and began "quiet quitting" on a large scale.

Of course the alternative is to foster sources of *intrinsic* motivation, within each member of the team, as the circuit's more sustainable source of power. As we'll explore in Part IV, this involves a clear, tangible sense of *mission*—one that can only thrive when every team member is free to express his own power and sense of purpose. That can only happen when the leader knows how to effectively turn the switch and keep it on.

Briefly, we'll complete the electrical circuit analogy, to inform our imaginations as we learn the practical steps of good communication. Every circuit has one or more lights, motors, or other functional points of activity. In our analogy, these represent the work—the productive tasks our team must undertake. Each one creates its own resistance to the current's flow, so it must be replenished from the original energy source.

In our crude analogy, that makes each member of the team a self-aware electron, as it were. Collectively, we must have enough force (voltage) and controlled flow (amperage) to complete the task. What makes us different from actual electrons, among many other differences, is that each of us must be aware of what others on the team are doing, and be mindful that our actions have consequences for everyone. A good leader knows this—and knows how to keep that awareness alive.

How to Connect

In Part I, we discussed the difficult leadership quality of vulnerability—knowing you don't have all the answers and being open to anyone else having them. This will serve you well when it comes to keeping communication flowing freely. In my own experience, I've always known the value of speaking one's mind. But I also know that many of us are uncomfortable doing so, for a host of reasons.

Over the years, a significant number of my employees have come from countries or cultures where, unless you were a boss of some sort, speaking out was simply not done. You were expected to just keep your mouth shut, do as you're told, and take your paycheck. Of course, this behavior is typical to vertical, hierarchical power structures everywhere, but it was especially true when I started my career in construction

So, at first, whenever I asked team members if they had questions or concerns, the usual response was silence. But as I recalled my "Vox Populi" experience, I persisted. I kept asking, because I really needed to know. I was not an all-seeing, all-knowing boss. In the construction business, threats to personal safety are always just around the corner, and I knew my people could see potential risks where I could not. Safety was an *imperative* that I knew others would relate to and, eventually, that others would be willing to talk about.

Gradually, as they realized I actually cared about their well-being, people began speaking more freely, which is when my second life-lesson kicked in. Just as I had promised my daughters I would not react negatively to anything they said, I kept to that standard with my team. It wasn't easy. Emotions and personal egos inevitably attached themselves to these discussions—just as they do today. But I resolved **never to take things personally**, and take their words at face value. Over time, my team began to trust I was on their side, especially when it came to safety. With practice, these exchanges started to involve issues beyond safety, as even those with less education came up with better ways to innovate and increase efficiency.

My construction company evolved this practice to a high degree—one that I recommend to businesses of any kind or size. Before the start of all projects, we hold an "all hands" meeting, in person. At these gatherings, everything is open for discussion—a metaphorical "Vox Populi" blackboard, if you will. The project's scope, timing, and goals are laid out, and everyone can speak their mind, without fear of repercussions. The rule, for everyone but especially for me and other team leaders, is never to talk **to** others, but always to talk **with** them, and to never take anything personally.

This dynamic also translates to our online Monday-morning status meetings and to our larger safety-themed gatherings. These generally happen twice a year, and have blossomed into social events for team members.

The hallmark of such events is an environment where anyone can express concerns without fear, but these principles are not limited to official meetings. As team members gained the confidence that they would be taken at their word, they became increasingly free to do so laterally, and daily. Today, aided by technology, team members are free to speak their minds in the moment, especially when unexpected or potentially dangerous situations arise. This was the case in 2014, when members of my team responded in the moment to a building collapse.

Lateral Movement

For companies to thrive, the concept of *lateral communication* must become more than an academic notion.[2] Unlike the situation in a vertical, hierarchical structure, communicating laterally does not have to go through an approval process, official or otherwise. Professionals at any place in the organization can reach out to anyone else, no matter what their title or position is. Today's technology makes this easy, in theory, but it does not just happen automatically. Anyone who has received a "reply to all" email on an obscure topic will attest that technology alone can lead to chaos and information overload, whether or not there is a formal process in place.[3]

The secret to truly effective lateral communication is a combination of a simple process (context, clarity, and brevity) and the human connection (empathy and active listening). As is the case in our status meetings, where anyone can offer their input without fear, someone (especially a leader) who receives a direct communication must never react in a negative way; they must take the words at face value and disregard the emotional baggage.

This applies to lateral messages received, of course, but also to messages *not* received. Think of all the times you sent out an email or text and did not receive an immediate reply, then drew your own premature conclusions. The chances are good that the recipient was not disrespecting you, especially if both of you have been communicating openly in the past.

As with planned meetings, having this level of communication on a one-to-one basis does not just happen automatically. Tools like Slack and Zoom, much less email and text, cannot generate the mutual vulnerability and trust required for fear-free communication. That responsibility lies with the leader who has the wisdom to turn on the switch, and the patience to keep the current flowing.

The Communicator's Toolbox

By now, you may be wondering if the leader's task of promoting fear-free communication, like vulnerability, is something only superheroes can do. Fortunately, that's not the case; mortals can do it. With a manageable level of patience and empathy, any leader can create such an environment. Even if there are some burned bridges in your history as a leader, these tools can help you rebuild them. The process begins by studying and applying the four basic skills we mentioned briefly in the previous chapter:

- *Invest time to know your employees.* This is worth the time it takes. Make it a priority to have extensive knowledge of your teammates' backgrounds, needs, and desires. For larger organizations, you'll need to be selective, of course, but in time, your other team leaders should develop the same leadership habit, getting to know their team members beyond just the tasks they perform for a paycheck. Ask them directly about career goals and aspirations. Ask what they want to get out of their job.

- A word of caution is needed here. If you use surveys or other "Vox Populi" equivalents, be sure you do so openly, honestly, and objectively.[4] Always follow up with anyone who answers. Nothing will create a cynical, transactional culture faster than saying nothing after asking for input.

- Keep in mind that the goal isn't to intrude or interrogate but to know your team members as human beings. If the connection is real, you'll gain foundational insights into their goals, strengths, and motivations. Once you know these things, you'll be able to apply the next basic skill.

- ***Match aptitude with suitable opportunities.*** As you continue to learn about your team players, make the connections between their development needs and opportunities for advancement. The fact is that they may not see many (or even any) of such opportunities—despite what self-help books and gurus may tell you. A hard-working employee is often too busy to see opportunities, or may feel that the opportunities are impractical. That means it's *your* job to constantly be on the lookout for things that can advance your employees' development and careers. Whenever these appear, ask yourself, *Whose growth and development would be most advanced if they pursued this opportunity?*

  - Traditional answers to the question "What opportunities will advance my career?" usually involve things like online certification, vocational training, and higher education.[5] Never dismiss these opportunities lightly, especially when the program is a good fit. An intelligent and promising young engineer I knew often had brilliant technical insights but had great difficulty expressing them in meetings. So, I helped him to enroll in some Dale Carnegie courses to elevate his communication skills.

- Sadly, the costs of higher education and other formal programs can limit these as practical opportunities. Even when costs are reasonable, they can require time that employees simply do not have. And often, a better alternative is to look *within* the company. Both Pew Research and McKinsey found that the lack of career development and advancement opportunities was the most common reason given for quitting a job.[6] So the obvious move is to be transparent and encouraging about any such opportunity.

- Opportunities like these need not be formal job openings. In our regular team meetings, suggestions on how to solve a particular construction problem often spawn an *ad hoc* team, creating an ideal environment for informal mentoring, stretch goals, and exercising skills that employees themselves didn't know they had. Going outside the traditional promotion cycle unlocks talent and catapults people to grow in different, unexpected directions.[7]

- Above all, your job is to be on the lookout for people who show an aptitude for a particular skill—even if it's unrelated to their current tasks. Once you start doing that on a consistent basis, you are ready to help them with the third basic skill.

- *Envision the desired results*. Throughout the process of matching people and opportunities, both you and those you lead need to have a clear picture of the desired benefits—both for the employee *and* for the organization. Once an opportunity has been assigned (and occasionally during the experience), do some "future-casting" with the employee. It's a process similar to the way AI projects are developed today.[8] The secret is to think through the potential benefits that *could* emerge if the opportunity were completed successfully. Always give strategic thought to the actions that must occur in order to maximize the probability of success—so you both know what "completed" really means.

  - When you help your teammate envision these results, always start with the ideal outcome. Much of that will come from what they are aiming to accomplish with their lives. You may think it unrealistic—from *your* perspective. However, it's important not to discourage them or impose your view of "the way it's always done." Remember, you need to exercise vulnerability and be open to the possibility that you don't know everything. Give your teammates the autonomy to explore possibilities on their own—and discover their own weaknesses as they gain new experience.

  - This process can be counter to typical career planning. Instead of starting from where they are now and working forward, future-casting is like telling a story backward. Starting at the future goal and working backward helps better define the steps to getting there and identify what needs to change.

· This does not have to be a formal or regimented process. In fact, it's usually best to keep it casual. With practice, it can become a perfectly normal part of your relationships. As it does, you'll find it easier and easier to practice the next phase.

· **_Provide consistent support_**. This skill is a natural outgrowth of the other three, but it requires something foundational from you. To fully support your employees, _you must genuinely desire their success_. In theory, of course we believe that their success will make the organization more successful. After all, studies have shown a positive correlation between employee satisfaction and engagement and good business outcomes.[9] But it's quite another matter to internalize the idea and put it into practice with flawed, flesh-and-blood human beings. In a transactional "I'm-the-boss" environment, it is next to impossible, but it can be done when you learn to think "outside the boss."

  · The secret, as mentioned earlier, is that you have presumably practiced the first three skills. You really know the aims of your employees. You've assigned them an opportunity that matches their skills. And you've worked with them to develop a clear picture of a successful outcome. If you've done all this, then you can't help but take a strong interest in their success.

· Support does not mean becoming a helicopter boss, micromanaging every detail—a classic symptom of a vertical, transactional style. Rather, your role is to be a reliable wingman, ready to provide support when needed, and offer encouragement when they fail. Stay involved by asking what support they need, removing barriers blocking their progress, and offering encouragement and guidance when they encounter roadblocks and bottlenecks.

The more you cultivate these four skills, the more you will see opportunities to open doors for others. In fact, other leaders on your team will often emulate this approach as they practice facilitating the flow of communication within their own spheres.

In my own experience, this level of open communication has had a remarkable but predictable side effect. Listening to and facilitating the aspirations of our employees, giving them autonomy over their own destiny, has created a climate of enjoyment and productivity. Consequently, our customers share that experience and enjoy it. Being heard and empowered is effectively a greater incentive than getting a break on price, which keeps them coming back for more.

CLOSING THE LOOP

Earlier in this chapter, I likened good communication to an electrical circuit, with the leader being the "switch" that keeps the current flowing through each of the connected members of an endeavor. One way to practice this metaphor in the real world is to always prioritize input during **and** at the end of every meeting.

- This practice can take several forms, but in my company, it typically goes like this: First, as a leader, I always expected my team members to be free to express concerns and alternative ideas—without fear of being ridiculed or marginalized. Of course, this put the onus on me and my fellow leaders to **not** react in a negative way, which takes patience and practice. Second, and perhaps most important, at the end of every meeting, we kept the circuit flowing. I always asked, "Is there anything we missed? Are there any issues or concerns we all need to know about?" The meeting ended, but communication remained open.

- When leaders really expect answers to these wide-open questions, and when each team member knows we'll take them seriously, without judgment, then the entire team knows they have value within the organization. They have authority and autonomy to act within their own area of skill, not just for a paycheck but to advance the mission of the entire team.

It's Not about the "Hero's Journey"

When I first began speaking and writing about communication, I naturally thought about heroic achievements, in myth or fiction and in real life. An audacious battle tactic, an epic quest, an unlikely sports triumph—they all share a common element. The hero or heroes are seldom alone. They have others around them who can anticipate their moves and come alongside when needed. We'd all like to imagine ourselves as Joan of Arc, Frodo Baggins, or Ted Lasso—the hero of the moment. But it's never about the solitary hero's journey. It's all about those we know and connect with and those who really know how to communicate.

If you want to lead an organization that flows like an Olympic skating pair, or the Miracle on Ice 1980 hockey team, if you prefer, then *you must take the fear out of communication*. Do this by making it a top priority. Be intentional about knowing your employees, respond quickly and openly (and do not take it personally) when they offer feedback and ideas, and make listening and support your priority.

The reason for fear-free communication is empowerment—first of your teammates and, by extension, your entire organization. It is by far the most effective path to unleashing creativity. It allows the leader to prove to each member the leader's investment in the team's success.

But it's up to you to take the first step—to lead by example. When it comes to communication, the leader (not the boss) cannot hide behind rules, mandates, and spreadsheets. By living these values for all to see, your employees are empowered to walk the talk as well. And your customers will see the difference.

CHAPTER 6

KEEPING THE CONVERSATION FLOWING

The world is full of talkers, but it is rare to find anyone who listens. And I assure you that you can pick up more information when you are listening than when you are talking.

—E. B. WHITE, *THE TRUMPET OF THE SWAN*

In theory, "measuring" one's conversational skills should be a routine matter, one involving basic literacy, comprehension, and mastery over basic technologies like the telephone, email, and Zoom. The rules of etiquette are also a factor. But the fact is that we can go through all the motions of having a conversation without ever communicating a thing. As George Bernard Shaw once said, "The single biggest problem in communication is the illusion that it has taken place."

As we noted in chapter 3, there is not a reliable way to objectively measure one's leadership qualities, even communication. But there are some good self-evaluation questions that, if considered thoughtfully, will give you a sense of where you are.

QUESTIONS ABOUT COMMUNICATION

Ask yourself the following questions, and take time to consider the answers you would have given years ago, in your leadership position right now, and in the not-so-distant future:

- When I ask people on my team if they have any questions, what proportion of them are silent? How many of them are off topic or argumentative?

- To what degree are members of your team made aware of your plans and strategy for your organization?

- To what degree do you solicit input from your team—on matters of immediate concern or on the organization's long-term strategy?

- When you inform a team member of an action performed poorly (or well), what is the typical response? How do you interpret that response? What action typically results from their response?

- When a team member criticizes (or praises) actions taken by you, or actions done with your approval, what is your typical response?

What are the consequences for that person?

- When communicating with individual team members, how much do you know about them, their capabilities, or their aspirations?

- To what degree do you seek out situations and opportunities that may be a good fit for the person with whom you are communicating?

Next, to reinforce the principles of good communication, let's look at two more hypothetical scenarios. Imagine yourself in a leadership position, at any level you choose, and consider the ways in which good communication would make a difference to the company's prospects. Of course, these particular kinds of companies may have many other challenges besides flawed communications. However, as you put yourself in their shoes, consider how many of these "other" problems might be solved—or at least contained—if its leader was proficient in fear-free communication.

Someone Will Be with You Shortly

Cable companies today have a less than stellar reputation. First appearing in the late 1940s, cable was initially the alternative to broadcast television in areas of relatively large populations with poor or inconvenient reception. Think of homes in low-lying regions, or apartment buildings where antennas were prohibited. Over the years, their reach grew to over 60 percent of US households by the early 1990s, but their reputation for service and transparency did not grow accordingly. In fact, cable companies consistently rank at or near the bottom of approval ratings among industries tracked by the American Customer Satisfaction Index.[1]

There are reasons for this. For years, cable companies have held absolute or near monopolies in their respective regions. They have a history of mergers, acquiring smaller fish in order to keep or expand their monopolies. There are well over seventy cable companies in the US today, but close to 70 percent of all industry revenue is concentrated in only a few large providers.

Each of these cable providers fought hard to protect their regional monopolies—aggregating tiers of more or less exclusive TV content, relentless lobbying, and eventually offering broadband internet over their extensive physical network. They've also been ruthless in cutting costs, especially when it comes to automation and offshore customer service. As most of us have experienced, getting to talk to a real person about a cable problem is frustrating and tedious.

I recognize the irony of a communications company that is known for its lack of good communication. But even with that reputation in mind, picture yourself in a leadership position at a hypothetical cable service provider. Clearly, it will be a steep climb to overcome years of people perceiving your company, justly or not, as a poor communicator, concerned only with the bottom line. But *imagine the types of communication that might be possible*, given such companies' enormous potential in terms of technical and institutional knowledge. Also, try to *imagine the long-term effects of actual open communication*, even if they take years to come to fruition.

In spite of (or maybe because of) all that baggage, consider the following:

· What, if anything, should be the repercussions if

someone in the organization voices an unpopular or unorthodox opinion, even if it is expressed in an angry or confrontational manner?

- How often should you hold project status meetings, and more importantly, who should attend and have a strong voice in such meetings? (Hint: they should not be management-only affairs.)

- Internet streaming services are a potential competitive threat. They are also relatively new and unpredictable, as are TV consumers' viewing habits. As a C-level executive, to what extent should *you* admit not knowing everything the future holds? Who else in the company might have good insights and creative responses to the problem? Do you have the means to hear them?

- How well do you know what transpires during a customer service call? How many such calls should you actually listen to?

- Most large cable companies employ some sort of artificial intelligence or machine learning to analyze customer input and/or generate responses to questions. To what extent should you rely on AI to make related business decisions? How would you safeguard against bias or overgeneralization in the use of chatbots or other AI tools?

- Most cable companies employ vast resources to install and maintain their networks and devices. This includes technicians with first-hand knowledge of customer issues. When, how, and how often should such individuals be made a real part of business decisions moving forward?

- Increasingly, government entities are pushing for expanded broadband coverage via public utility districts' use of fiber-optic networks. As a C-level executive or company spokesperson, how should you communicate with governments and the people they represent? What are some mutually beneficial goals inherent in such actions?

Cable companies are not alone in facing customer and employee outrage, often amplified by social media. Large, powerful companies are easy targets for criticism, earned and unearned. Too often, the response is punitive and/or self-protective—and devoid of meaningful communication. But as we saw in chapter 5, some companies have responded differently, valuing competent humility and transparent communication as a means of achieving success.

The Retail Revival

Selling physical goods to customers is a business as old as civilization itself. Retail markets coincide more or less with the invention of money, a much better method than trading chickens for pomegranates. They have always been a hallmark of humanity, but the *nature* of retail itself is changing constantly—and at greater and greater velocity. While it's still possible to browse and shop for bargains at an outdoor bazaar, the history and number of retail sales advances are too numerous and complex to mention in any detail.[2]

The communication demands on retail business are enormous. Think of all the people and organizations with which you must exchange information. There are the customers, of course, but a friendly, in-person exchange at a physical store is just one of countless possible two-way communications. Then there is the myriad assortment of manufacturers, wholesalers, and distributors, most of whom you will never meet in person—save for the service reps (online or on the phone) and delivery drivers (in person, for brief moments). Finally, there are all the people within your retail organization, from the brand-new salesperson or stock mover, fresh out of school, to the senior managers, and everyone in between. Each one has the right to expect clear communication throughout their busy day. They need to hear one another, and be heard.

Now, multiply this demand a hundredfold for that uniquely modern phenomenon—the retail chain. Since the mid-nineteenth century, everything-you-need department stores like Marshall Field's (now Macy's) have evolved into shopping malls, supercenters, and big-box stores, each with its own massive network of communications needs. Online retail is no exception. Even for behemoths like Amazon, and for traditional retail chains adding e-commerce to their repertoire, mastering complex communication is essential.

Now, no matter how much or how little experience you have in the retail world (other than shopping), put yourself in the shoes of a senior executive of a hypothetical retail chain. Consider the following facets of communication that will make or break your business:

- Retail chains require frequent meetings for their marketing and sales strategy teams. Their HR, logistics, and planning departments must also meet to ensure smooth operations. Who should attend such meetings besides those whose titles include "marketing," or "sales," etc.?

- How are the opinions and observations of those outside one's department or sphere received—if they are even heard?

- So much communication within retail chains involves complex data on products, sales, and customer trends. How can you really know what the data means—and is there anyone who can help explain it?

- Retail customers today expect to exchange information and opinions about your company and its products in multiple ways and on multiple channels and platforms. How should you communicate your message, and how should you listen to theirs? (Be as specific as you like.)

- When a criticism of your company or its products becomes a public scandal, for whatever reason, is your first response to address the public relations issue or to find a solution to the original problem?

- In general, how do members of your company share their concerns—and how are they treated personally if they express those concerns negatively?

In retail, the default mode of operating is *transactional*—someone pays you for a product that they need or want. But we know the ideal is more than that. Deep down, we know that buying something has a *relational* component, one that is foundational to customer loyalty and goodwill. Retail customers, employees, and executives alike share the deeper need for human connection and purpose that is fostered by honest and transparent communication. It may be "only" a bag of groceries or a new shirt, but what happens in a store has a deeper meaning. And the retailer who embraces it will thrive.

PART III

TRUST

CHAPTER 7

TAKING A LEAP

*It takes twenty years to build a reputation
and five minutes to ruin it. If you think about that,
you'll do things differently.*
—WARREN BUFFETT

Trust has long been recognized as one of a leader's most valuable assets. For members of your team, trust is *their* well-founded belief in your integrity, ability, and character. It's also *your* belief in theirs. Trust is always a two-way relationship. This is true of sound personal relationships, of course, but it's also the true foundation of any successful organization—no matter its size or purpose.

Trust cannot be based on words; it depends on the actual behavior of leaders and fellow team members. It cannot be faked or fabricated. Saying one thing and doing the opposite is the diametric opposite of trust. It must be earned by deliberate, persistent action. And if it is broken, it is exponentially harder to restore.

> **TRUST—THE WELL-FOUNDED BELIEF IN ONE'S INTEGRITY, ABILITY, AND CHARACTER—IS THE TRUE FOUNDATION OF ANY SUCCESSFUL ORGANIZATION.**

The benefits of trust cannot be overstated. It provides an environment that gives employees freedom to take risks and to express their ideas freely, without fear of retribution. It motivates them to communicate more freely, as we explored in chapters 4 and 5, and encourages them to innovate.

When employees and leaders alike have reason to trust one another, they are free to make their organization (and themselves) successful. People in high-trust companies tend to have more satisfaction with their own lives, more engagement, and *much* more energy at work, compared with people in low-trust companies. They also have far less stress, less burnout, and fewer sick days, according to research cited in *Harvard Business Review* (*HBR*).[1]

The same article pointed to some of the neurological bases for trust among human beings. One of the brain's messaging chemicals, the hormone oxytocin, is what tells us that another animal—or in this case, another human—is safe to approach. It has a long evolutionary history, presumably because those who produced it in sufficient measure were more likely to reproduce. It is believed to be part of the reason why we have relationships and form communities.[2]

The *HBR* article also noted that certain management behaviors, such as recognizing excellence and giving people discretion in how they work, stimulated oxytocin production and generated trust. Not surprisingly, two other behaviors described earlier in this book—showing vulnerability and sharing information broadly—also increased oxytocin levels and generated trust.

Trust is driven by several important factors, which we'll explore in chapter 8. But before we dig deeper into *how* to implement trust as a core leadership value, we need to know more about *why* we trust some things implicitly, and when we need to earn that trust.

Implicit and Explicit Trust

Human beings are born trusting. We have no choice; we're more helpless at birth than most other mammals. Thankfully, most parents and other caregivers protect us as well as they can, giving us a sense of security that serves as a foundation for many of our best attributes as people.

Such trust is *implicit* in nature. It literally goes without saying and without spending a lot of conscious reasoning. We trust that morning will follow night and waking up will follow sleep. We trust that our bodies will function, more or less, without our close attention. Absent evidence to the contrary, we trust that random people we meet on the street will act normally, more or less, without causing us any harm. As discussed in chapter 2, psychologist Daniel Kahneman noted that we have subconscious ways of evaluating if a stranger is trustworthy or not, based on subtle visual cues and our evolutionary past.[3] But as he also pointed out, our automatic responses, while often necessary, can also be the *wrong* responses. Our "gut feeling" that so-and-so is trustworthy, or that such-and-such is a safe course of action, may lead us to disappointment and harm.

> ## ACT IN WAYS THAT FOSTER EXPLICIT TRUST, AND DO SO WITH SUCH FREQUENCY THAT TRUST BECOMES IMPLICIT.

The answer is not to cultivate a cynical mistrust of everyone and everything. The world already has plenty of that particular toxin. The answer is to act in ways that foster explicit trust, and to do so with such frequency and conscious effort that trust becomes implicit.

For a leader to develop trust within his organization, he must spend considerable time and effort trusting in his team and acting in their best interests. That means looking for ways to match their abilities and aspirations with opportunities that benefit both them and the entire organization. It does not happen overnight. There is no course to take or app you can download to cultivate trust in others. You must put in the work to earn it.

* * * *

Think about some of the things you do that involve implicit trust in something, in someone, or an organization made up of some-ones, none of whom you know personally. You get into your car, or step into an elevator, and press a button or turn a key. You have never met the people who designed and built the technology; you likely don't know well the people who maintain it. And yet, you normally don't think twice. You assume that the car will move forward or that the elevator will go safely to where you want to go.

Take some more pressing examples, where your immediate choices are limited. Suppose you're involved in an accident, or you experience sudden physical pain, and an EMT arrives, or perhaps you have someone take you to the emergency room. It's unlikely that you'll know the EMT or the doctor personally, and yet you believe they can help you. This is more the case if you haven't had a bad experience with a healthcare provider (more on that later), but the normal, unthinking response is to trust them. They know what they're doing.

Take another example, where you *do* have choices but your default response is one of implicit trust. If you have a child in daycare, you're likely to have researched your provider and met the provider in person. But in all likelihood, you won't know everything there is to know about the people taking care of your child. Despite that, when you drop off your child, you believe that everything will be fine. All parents worry about their children, of course, but in typical routine situations like this, having implicit trust is perfectly normal.

There's one more example, which is more complicated. When you board an airplane, it is highly unlikely that you will know any of the people involved in making that plane safe, but it's also very likely that air travel is your only practical option. So, out of necessity and because there's simply not enough time to examine everyone and everything involved, you calmly board the plane, as almost three million US passengers do every day, trusting that all will be well.[4]

Of course there are circumstances that erode such trust, as we will see, but it's still a normal, often unquestioned response to everyday situations. This is necessary in today's complicated world. We literally don't have enough time to investigate or research every possibility—to prove that every situation is safe. Implicit trust is a survival mechanism, allowing us to go on with our day.

So, what makes people think that things will be OK in these

situations? The reality is that something *can* go wrong, at least in theory. However, if the chances of that happening are small, and if the situation is largely outside our control, we tend to trust the outcome implicitly.*

The thing to remember is that when a situation is outside our control, implicit trust is perfectly normal. **But when we have a choice, the equation changes.** Whenever we have a vested interest in the outcome of a given situation—whether in short-term situations or over the course of one's entire career—trust must be *explicit*, and it must be earned.

> ## WHENEVER WE HAVE A VESTED INTEREST IN THE OUTCOME OF A SITUATION, TRUST MUST BE EXPLICIT, AND IT MUST BE EARNED.

Trust is not just a part of our nature as busy human beings. It is critical to effective leadership, and to the ultimate success of any endeavor. As we will see, it is the bond of trust between leaders and their team that keeps them functioning in difficult situations. It's also the key to winning and retaining strong relationships with customers. But when that trust is broken, it is painfully hard to restore.

Trust Earned and Lost

Let's take one of the examples of trust we mentioned earlier:

---

*I'm not suggesting that people who fear possible bad outcomes are wrong or being unduly obsessive or paranoid. The world is not always a safe place. I'm just saying that implicit trust is often how we make it through the day.

commercial airline travel. Widespread trust was not always a given. Before federal-level regulation began in earnest in the 1930s, there was an average of one fatal accident for every million miles travelled.[5] If that trend held true today, we'd be having about 7,000 fatal airline accidents every year! But the trend is dramatically otherwise. Despite regulation changes, or maybe even because of them, there are now 0.0007 fatal accidents per million miles—or 0.05 fatal accidents per million flights.[6] By one estimate, the passenger vehicle death rate per 100 million miles is almost 600 times higher than it is for scheduled airlines.[7]

Part of this impressive trend was due to one company in particular: Boeing. For many years prior to the 1990s, the venerable aircraft and aerospace manufacturer was renowned for its meticulous engineering and adherence to safety standards. For years, public trust in the company's products stayed at an all-time high, contributing to our collective belief in the safety of air travel. But this trust was undermined following the 1997 merger with McDonnell Douglas. According to former engineers, Boeing began to skimp on detailed (and expensive) safety and training requirements, and increasingly focused on speed, cost, and shareholder returns.[8] This all came to a head with the scandals involving the Boeing 737 MAX.

Since 2018, these planes have earned much public ill will, with incidents ranging from fatal crashes to alarming equipment failures and FAA-mandated groundings. Many have taken Boeing to task for its corporate shift from safety-first to shareholder value, with some wondering if the company's reputation can even be salvaged.[9] In fact, at least one travel app has added a feature that allows users to exclude specific types of planes, like the 737 MAX, from their search for flights.

Clearly, Boeing has lost the trust of many, and will find it exceedingly hard to win back that trust. The company itself is not likely to go away; after all, it is one of only two global airplane manufacturers. But for the foreseeable future, it will likely be a hard place to work for many people.

It's All about the People

But here's where it gets interesting. Despite this loss of trust in Boeing, most people still have trust in air travel itself. A recent AP-NORC poll found that 71 percent of US adults consider planes a safe method of travel.[10] But the details of the survey are important to our understanding of trust.

> TRUST IN INDIVIDUAL LEADERS AND THEIR ABILITIES IS FAR MORE POWERFUL THAN THE ENTITIES TO WHICH THEY BELONG.

Notably, in the same poll, the trust numbers were significantly higher for the *people* in the industry—pilots and air traffic controllers—than for *entities* like airlines, manufacturers, and especially the government. This explains why the trust level remains high, on average, but it also points to an important aspect of trust.

Trust in individual leaders and their abilities is far more powerful than the entities to which they belong. Trusted leaders always effect change, and eventually raise the trust level of the organizations they lead. Organizations alone, no matter how noble their mission statements, cannot instill that trust.

As a vivid case in point, think about the circumstances surrounding the famous 2009 aviation incident now known as the "Miracle on the Hudson." After a sudden catastrophic loss of power in both engines on US Airways Flight 1549, the pilot, Chesley "Sully" Sullenberger, managed to land his stricken plane on the Hudson River without a single loss of life. As his personal account details, the incident justly highlights his competence and calm, but it also serves as a portrait of trust—especially the kind of trust that can exist among members of a team.[11]

> ## FOR A LEADER TO ENGENDER TRUST, HE MUST HAVE GOOD REASON TO TRUST HIMSELF AND HIS ABILITIES.

First, Sullenberger clearly trusted himself and his first officer, Jeffrey Skiles. For a leader to engender trust, he must have good reason to trust himself, his abilities, and the abilities of his team. In Sullenberger's 2019 interview with *Inc.* magazine,[*] he described how they communicated with each other during the 208 seconds between the bird strike and their emergency landing on the Hudson:

> He and I were able to collaborate wordlessly by knowing intuitively in this developing crisis what we should do to help the other, based on our own long experience. Had Jeff not also had 20,000 hours of flying time like I did, had he not been a captain before, had he not been so experienced, he wouldn't have known either to do that or how to do that. So he made an important suggestion at several

---

* The entire online video is well worth watching: "Captain Sully's Minute-by-Minute Description of the Miracle on the Hudson." YouTube, March 6, 2019. https://www.youtube.com/watch?v=w6EblErBJqw.

points in the flight. He was silently cheering me on as I made each decision, but ready to intervene, to check my performance if he thought I was making an error.

Second, he trusted in those who had invested in his training over the years—and in the nature of the training itself. In the same interview, Sullenberger described his vivid, visceral responses during the first moments after impact. But he also described how his training kicked in.

> Because I had learned my craft so well, I knew my airplane and my profession so intimately, I could set clear priorities. And so I chose to do only the highest-priority items, and then I had the discipline to ignore everything I did not have time to do as being only distractions and potential detriment to our performance.

Third, he trusted the others on his flight crew to do their jobs in a crisis. Trust is always a two-way street. When he spoke his brief PA announcement, "This is the captain; brace for impact," he knew that all three flight attendants would follow their training and prepare all the passengers quickly.

> And immediately, even through that armored cockpit door, I could hear the two flight attendants in front, Donna and Sheila, and I'm sure Doreen in the back was doing the same, begin shouting their commands in unison to the passengers. "Brace, brace, brace. Heads down, stay down."

Hearing those words that day encouraged me. It comforted me to know that by saying the few words I had, but choosing the right words, I had literally gotten my crew on the same page and that if I could find a way to deliver this aircraft to the surface intact, it would float long enough for the flight attendants to evacuate the passengers.

Trust was evident in abundance once the plane had landed safely. The crew and fellow passengers helped everyone exit, while a small fleet of boats converged to rescue everyone waiting on the wings. As the 2016 film adaptation of Sullenberger's book recounts, those rescues required many acts of individual trust— by and between complete strangers.

It took only twenty-four minutes from the moment of impact to safely remove every passenger from the plane. That meant the entire event, from the plane's takeoff to the river rescue was less than a half hour!

The crisis of Flight 1549 was dramatic and poignant in ways that we seldom experience in the day-to-day work of leading a team. It does provide some important leadership lessons, however. The first is that *crises will always occur*, usually at inconvenient times and in the midst of other pressing deadlines. They will test our behavior—to prove whether or not our principles of vulner-ability, communication, and trust are real or just words. And as with most crises, they won't give us time to think everything through calmly.

This raises the second lesson: *trust needs to become a lifetime habit*, as do all the other principles in this book. Sullenberger's and Skiles's 20,000 hours of experience made their actions—and their mutual trust—essentially instinctive and automatic. You and your team members cannot earn trust overnight. It takes practice, perhaps not 20,000 hours' worth, but certainly a conscious, dedicated effort, a willingness to learn from mistakes (i.e., vulnerability), and a commitment to ongoing, open communication. Many of your people will not want to trust you at first—nor you them—but with practice they will.

> ## THE ESSENCE OF TRUST, AND OF BEING TRUSTED, ALWAYS COMES DOWN TO PEOPLE—NOT ORGANIZATIONAL MECHANICS.

The final lesson is that it's always about who you are as a human being, not as a boss. ***The essence of trust, and of being trusted, always comes down to the people involved***, not to the mechanics of our organizational structures. After Sullenberger's amazing feat, he and Skiles faced a difficult official investigation. He had not acted "by the book." His actions were questioned and challenged to the point where he even doubted himself—wondering if he had been too reckless. He was vindicated in the end, but all too often, organizational structure is the enemy of trust, or at least a hindrance to its exercise.

That is not to say that structure is unimportant. It's a necessary part of life, but it's not what makes you an effective leader. As I said earlier in the book, *if you understand modern business techniques, then you're merely a technician, but if you truly understand people, then you're a leader.*

Leading by Example

Building trust is never an easy matter. Our own human nature too often gets in the way. We have a tendency to pull back and go into self-preservation mode—as do our fellow team members. It's only natural, which is why so many business leaders end up following a traditional hierarchical "I'm-the-boss-so-do-what-I-say" style. Naturally, this only perpetuates mistrust. So, if you really want your people to trust you—and each other by extension—there are some things you need to practice on a regular basis.

Above all, *be human*. If you don't have the answer to a problem, just admit it. As we explored in Part I, competent humility and vulnerability are not only powerful leadership attributes; they also just make sense! Everyone you work with knows you're not some all-knowing superhero. They will trust you, and that trust will increase, if *they* know that *you* know it too.

> ## WHEN YOU ARE ABLE TO COMMUNICATE TRANSPARENTLY, THE RESULTING INCREASE IN TRUST WILL ENABLE YOU TO FIND ANSWERS TOGETHER.

In my own experience, allowing myself to be real with my employees has earned enormous trust over the years, opening up a tradition of fear-free dialogue. As it has done for me, when you are all able to communicate transparently, the resulting increase in trust will enable you to find answers together.

Second, *practice stepping in as a player* (and a coach). Of course you cannot do everyone's job for them, and there will always be jobs they're better at than you. (The latter helps on the humility front, by the way.) But you should never ask people to do something you're not willing to do yourself. Whether it's covering for someone on a project, helping them work through a decision-making process, or helping remove an obstacle they failed to notice, they will know and trust that you have their interests at heart.

Third, learn to regularly and sincerely ***celebrate accomplishments***. This doesn't mean a passing mention in the company newsletter, or a free promotional gadget. Whether it's meeting a group goal or an individual achievement, everyone counts and everyone values being recognized publicly for it. Mutual trust stems from the confidence that all team members can thrive in their respective roles, be recognized for their talents, and be given opportunity to grow. This is amazingly fertile ground where team members can learn to support and advocate for themselves and others.

> ## MUTUAL TRUST STEMS FROM THE CONFIDENCE THAT ALL TEAM MEMBERS CAN THRIVE IN THEIR RESPECTIVE ROLES.

The fourth practice should be obvious but too often is not: ***love your craft***. Presumably, you are (or want to be) a leader in your chosen field because there's something about it that resonates with you.[*] When your team knows how much you love what you do, they tend to get excited too. That connection fosters trust because they know you aren't acting based on ulterior motives.

---

[*] Making more money doesn't count. If that's your only goal, then you're probably in the wrong field.

It also fosters more creativity and joy in the work itself—which translates into better results, and proof that their trust was not misplaced. Because we're not living and working in a vacuum, your unapologetic passion for what you do will help create a workplace in which your team can take collective pride.

All this takes time—not to mention regular practice, patience, and regular helpings of courage. Trust is a hard-won skill, but once you build it, I can guarantee it will engage and motivate your team.

The View from the Air

The sport of skydiving has some powerful elements that will help us imagine the complexities of trust while safely on the ground. Think about all the people, known and unknown, who are involved in one's jump from a plane. First, there's yourself. Whether you're doing it for fun, for the adrenaline rush, or out of necessity if the plane is going down, it takes courage to do something so audacious. In wartime, paratroopers knew it was a good tactic, but it still required bravery. As a sport, each attempt demands something extra from you.

Then, there's the matter of your own preparedness. Do you trust that you're in good enough condition, and that you've learned what there is to know about doing this safely? Beyond yourself, you also need to trust that your instructor was knowledgeable and communicated clearly.

Going a bit deeper, you need to trust others, like the plane's pilot and crew, the meteorologist who gave the thumbs up, the company that made the plane (and the parachute!) and the maintenance crew that kept things running. Above all, you need to trust the person who packed your parachute.

Which brings us to a story, author unknown but generally

believed to be true, that is worth mentioning here in the context of skydiving—and trust.[12]

> Inspirational speaker Charles Plumb had been a US Navy jet pilot in Vietnam. After seventy-five combat missions, his plane was destroyed by a surface-to-air missile. He ejected and parachuted into enemy territory. He was captured and spent six years in a North Vietnamese prison.
>
> One day long afterward, when Plumb and his wife were sitting in a restaurant, a man from another table approached him and said, "You're Plumb! You flew jet fighters in Vietnam from the *Kitty Hawk*. You were shot down!"
>
> "How in the world did you know that?" asked Plumb.
>
> "I packed your parachute," the man replied. Plumb gasped in surprise and gratitude. The man pumped his hand and said, "I guess it worked!" "It sure did," Plumb assured him. "If your chute hadn't worked, I wouldn't be here today."

In Plumb's public speeches since that time, he includes a question to the audience, "Who's packing your parachute?"—a powerful call to recognize those who are unseen but play important roles in our lives. But the story also reminds us that those we trust—and the actions they undertake—may not be obvious.

CHAPTER 8

BUILDING BONDS THAT LAST

Few things help an individual more than to place responsibility upon him, and to let him know that you trust him.

—BOOKER T. WASHINGTON

It should go without saying that the "how" part of building trust depends heavily on a leader's willingness to be vulnerable and transparent through his practice of fear-free communication, which we covered in the first half of the book. The concepts are interrelated, but the *practical* aspects of creating and maintaining trust deserve our full attention.

When members of a team trust one another to look out for each other's well-being, and especially when a leader has earned such trust, there are enormous, tangible benefits. Trust reduces or eliminates costly micromanagement. It builds individual confidence in each team member's own abilities. It inspires greater innovation and a willingness to be seen for one's true potential. Most of all, mutual trust increases productive responses to challenges, turning costly mistakes into long-term and ultimately profitable learning experiences.

The process of establishing and maintaining trust is a long one that will require a lifetime of practice, but there are some guiding principles that will help you succeed. The first is to ***trust in people more than they trust themselves***. This may seem counterintuitive, especially if you have experienced a betrayal of trust more than once. But if you know them and their potential, you'll find it easier to navigate your reservations and stay with it.

> **TRUST IN PEOPLE MORE THAN THEY TRUST THEMSELVES.**

Trusting your people does not mean doing so blindly. Providing structure and context is critical, as is a clear understanding of the job requirements. But beware of setting a structure heavily laden with transactional conditions and warnings. If you structure it well, without preconditions, your people will eventually understand the value of those parameters—and become part of their evolution.

A $50,000 INVESTMENT

The value of trust in people, despite their mistakes, cannot be underestimated. Some years ago, a magazine publishing executive—and a well-regarded inspirational speaker—recounted an incident involving a very junior editor who had made a serious mistake, despite the experience that had warranted her new position. When she owned up to her mistake, he noted that her poor judgment had cost one of his magazines over $50,000 in revenue.

Expecting to be fired on the spot, she was shocked at his response. "Why in the world would I fire you? I just spent $50,000 on your education!" That evidence of his confidence and trust in her resulted in her becoming, in his words, the best editor he had ever worked with.

To be sure, a decision to trust someone, even before you're sure of the outcome, never feels comfortable, especially at first. Trust is like a chain built one link at a time. It involves a series of *explicit* behaviors that eventually leads to *implicit* belief in that person's reliability, her care for others' well-being, and her support for the overall mission.

TRUST MEANS HAVING CONFIDENCE IN SOMEONE'S CHARACTER AND INTENTIONS, DESPITE NOT KNOWING THE OUTCOME.

But the fact is that trust is not really a chicken-and-egg dilemma. You can never be 100 percent certain of any outcome. So, true trust means having confidence in someone's character and intentions, despite not knowing the outcome in advance. It is built not by demanding guaranteed outcomes but by being open to those whose character can be relied upon.

Trust is a commitment to ongoing employee development, a decision to stay the course, despite mistakes made along the way. It requires confidence in one's direction or mission, which we'll discuss in Part IV, as a point of reference to lean on in times of doubt and turmoil. Trust has no season; it's not dependent on the emotional or circumstantial "weather" of the moment. It demands a serious amount of fortitude, along with the intelligence to make course corrections when you or anyone else strays off the path.

How to Get There

Paul Zak's seminal article *The Neuroscience of Trust* provides some initial clues on how to cultivate greater trust.[1] One is to ***recognize and celebrate excellence.*** As we discussed in the previous chapter, this cannot be rote or routine, such as a passing mention in a company newsletter. It also cannot be a hollow gesture, such as an "employee of the month" plaque. Instead, true recognition should take the form of public acknowledgement, during the regular course of business, that the person's actions have contributed something truly meaningful. It could be a safety improvement, a customer service "rescue," or a boost in revenue or profitability. Whatever the accomplishment, publicly recognizing its value tells the employee (and everyone else) that she is valued for her abilities. The resulting increase in trust is directly proportional to the sincerity of your recognition.

EVERYBODY MATTERS

In 1975, Bob Chapman assumed control of his late

father's company, Barry-Wehmiller, a provider of (among many other things) packaging equipment and paper processing solutions. Originally founded in 1885, the St. Louis–based firm has acquired over eighty other companies since 1987, and now boasts revenue of over three billion dollars annually.

But the company's reputation is more notable for Chapman's leadership principles centered on creating a caring, people-centric culture.[2] The result is a high-trust organization that effectively recognizes top performers in each of the divisions it owns.

Chapman and his team initiated a program in which employees at each plant nominate an outstanding peer each year. The winner is kept secret until announced to everyone, and the facility is closed on the day of the celebration. The chosen employee's family and close friends are invited to attend (without tipping off the winner), and their entire staff joins them. Plant leaders kick off the ceremony by reading nominating letters about the winner's contributions. The celebration ends with the presentation of a favorite perk—the keys to a sports car that the winner gets to drive for a week.

Although the recognition isn't immediate, it is tangible and, if all goes to plan, unexpected. More importantly, it is both personal and public. By having employees help pick the winners, the company leaders give everyone, not just those at the top, a meaningful say in what constitutes excellence.

Recognition need not always be a major event. A simple job-well-done remark can often suffice. The key is to let the person—and those around him—see that his efforts have earned your respect and trust. Over time, if the recognition is real, that trust will be reciprocated.

Another trust-building practice is to **_give your people greater autonomy_**. This means giving them more discretion in how they work, allowing them the opportunity to try new things, and even letting them choose to become involved in projects that appeal to them personally. They are still accountable for their choices, but if the projects are in line with the mission, the increase in mutual trust is well worth stepping away from intensive micromanagement.

Personal autonomy matters a lot more than we realize. Being trusted to figure things out is a big motivator. According to a 2014 study by Citigroup and LinkedIn, nearly half of those surveyed would forego a 20 percent raise over greater control over how they work.[3] Since then, the work disruptions of COVID have made this dilemma even more acute, as many workers resist return-to-the-office directives. Their desire for more autonomy is also evidenced by the "quiet quitting" phenomenon, where workers only do the bare minimum required.

Worker autonomy has proven benefits, especially when it comes to innovation. In a 2017 study, growth in the development of new products was connected to firms providing their employees with greater time, freedom, and independence.[4] An earlier study found that job autonomy acts as a buffer against work–life conflicts, leading to dissatisfaction and turnover.[5] Simply put, granting greater autonomy is a leader's public expression of trust—one that produces not only greater satisfaction and engagement but also an increased likelihood that you will be trusted in return.

Zak's article on the neuroscience of trust also highlights two practices covered earlier in this book. One is **open communication**—keeping everyone informed about your company's goals, strategies, tactics, and progress. As we discussed in chapter 5, communication is like an electric circuit, allowing each element to perform its function smoothly. The other is **vulnerability**. When a leader admits he doesn't know everything, or asks for help rather than just demanding compliance, trust and cooperation increase. Being vulnerable signals that a leader is secure, willing to engage with everyone to achieve goals.

Vulnerability is something you can express only if you are available to your team members to the extent it is possible. **Accessibility** makes you relatable; it is the way to build face-to-face trust. Physical presence is fundamental to creating engagement. Have you ever worked for a leader whose presence you only felt through emails and whose face you wouldn't recognize in a lineup? Even if it can only happen via Zoom or FaceTime, nothing can replace face-to-face interaction.

It is important for leaders to meet their people at "ground level" by showing genuine curiosity not only in their work for the company but also in their interests, opinions, and beliefs. It's not something you can fake. If done out of a real desire to know, it fosters a sense of psychological safety and a work environment that creates more and lasting productivity.

The Source of Engagement

Well before COVID and the "quiet quitting" phenomenon, most American workers were not engaged in their jobs. According to a

2011 Gallup poll, 71 percent were "not engaged" or were "actively disengaged" in their work.[6] That alarming number has remained consistent, leaving only about one-third of employees emotionally connected and enthusiastic. As Gallup and many others point out, this has a decisive, negative effect on their companies' overall performance. Without positive engagement, employees have no reason to trust their leaders or even their fellow team members. They are far less likely to be productive, and far more likely to quit—quietly or otherwise.

To counter this, the typical hierarchical response is to entice workers with special perks or, as a last resort, with pay increases. (Some have also resorted to punitive measures against quiet quitters, which have largely failed.) But the problem with this carrot-and-stick approach is that it does little to foster trust or job satisfaction. In fact, research suggests that monetary rewards are not as motivational as bosses think they are, and that they may actually be *demotivating*.[7]

> **EMPLOYEES AT LOW-TRUST ORGANIZATIONS ARE MORE LIKELY TO WITHHOLD INFORMATION AND HOARD RESOURCES BECAUSE THEY DON'T FEEL SAFE SHARING THEM.**

Salaries and perks cannot counteract a low-trust environment, where employees are just told to do their jobs without question and with no regard for their interest in or competence to perform the work. Employees at low-trust organizations are often bogged down by office politics and internal conflicts. They are more likely to withhold information and hoard resources because they don't feel safe sharing them. As a result, decision-making is slower and less effective.

At a time when distrust seems to be the default, fostering a high-trust organization has never been so important—and it starts with leadership.

* * * *

In their 2023 MIT Sloan report, authors Ashley Reichheld and Amelia Dunlop describe their novel platform for measuring four elements of trust in the workplace and elsewhere.[8] By measuring a company's performance on each of these aspects—humanity, transparency, capability, and reliability—leaders can get a view of both how well they are trusted (or not) and why. As we will learn, it can also help us understand what needs to be done to increase that trust.

The open-source survey consists of four statements, each asking the employee to rate their agreement on a one-to-seven-point scale:

Humanity: My employer demonstrates empathy and kindness toward me.

Transparency: My employer uses straightforward and plain language to share information, motives, and decisions that matter to me.

Capability: My employer creates a good work experience for me and provides the resources I need to do my job well.

Reliability: My employer consistently and dependably delivers on the commitments it made to me.

Some interesting facts have emerged from Deloitte's use of this survey. Few organizations received high scores in all four areas, while some scored higher in some areas but lower in others—indicating potential blind spots in a company's trust-building strategy. In further studying the responses and subsequent behavior of over 15,000 employees, the research revealed some valuable insights for leaders, such as the following:

- Those who gave their employers high ratings on *reliability* are 40 percent more likely to share personal information.

- Those who gave their employers high scores on *humanity* or *transparency* are 50 percent more likely to go out of their way to optimize their work or take on additional responsibility.

- Those who gave their employers high scores on *capability* are 60 percent more likely to learn new skills on their own to improve their work.

Of course, these findings show correlation, not causation. But the fact remains that high-trust work environments are the likely places for employees to excel. When employers acknowledge that *employees are humans first*, not transactional resources, they will realize the long-term value in meeting their team members' human needs and earning their trust. Here's what the survey authors concluded:

"The payoff will be more trusting employees and the potential of all that flows from this: greater staff engagement, less absenteeism and turnover, higher productivity, and—perhaps most important—an elevated work experience for everyone, from the front lines to the C-suite."

Building a High-Trust Workplace

The Deloitte survey provides a useful template for leaders. Whether or not their company actually conducts the survey, it offers four distinct areas of focus on how they can create a workplace where trust is paramount.

Building the *empathy* component of trust is difficult for many leaders, especially in a workplace filled with millions of micro-demands on our time. Think about how hard it is to put yourself in someone's shoes when interruptions and distractions are the everyday norm.

Exercising empathy is also hard for leaders with so-called Type A personalities—competitive, highly organized, time-conscious, and driven to explore and learn. They can easily become impatient with those who have different motivations or who take longer than they think it should to understand something. But when that impatience signals, rightly or wrongly, that a leader cares more about the task than about the person, that person will trust less and resist even more.

> ## SEEING FROM OTHERS' PERSPECTIVE ALLOWS YOU TO LEARN WHO THEY ARE AND HOW THEY CAN DO BETTER.

Part of the problem with empathy is that it's often confused with *sympathy*, although the two are strikingly different concepts. *Empathy involves feeling what another person feels; sympathy involves understanding what they feel but from your own perspective.* You may have thoughts about how someone feels (sympathy), but they could easily be superficial—if not completely wrong. You might be sympathetic and still be passing judgment or offering unsolicited advice. But when you see things from others' perspectives (empathy), you can learn a lot. You don't have to agree with their views, but you're less likely to judge and more likely to learn who they are and how they can do better—for themselves and for their company.

Empathy and the trust it generates do not happen overnight. It begins with some simple habits, such as ignoring your phone, or putting it away, when talking with others on your team. Prioritizing people over distractions will change the quality of your interactions, increasing your ability to foster trust.

Another crucial step in exercising your empathy habits is the difficult process of *active listening*—paying attention not only to the words being spoken but also to the speaker's body language, their tone of voice, and other nonverbal cues. This goes beyond paying full attention. It requires handling your own emotions—remaining calm, nonjudgmental, and slow to convey annoyance or boredom. Above all, active listening requires you to convey your *actual* interest and comprehension, both verbally and nonverbally.[9]

There are many opportunities to practice this. In meetings

or other group settings, prioritize making sure others get what they need—rather than focusing on your requirements. Facilitate others' contributions, and do not disengage until everyone else is clear on their part in meeting a goal. It takes practice—and a concerted effort to ignore phones and other distractions. As with every other trust-building practice, that will mean leading by example and ignoring your own phone.

Exercising that level of empathy and trustworthiness is only possible when you are *present* and visible to everyone. Displaying employee photos or showing up at employee recognition events does not accomplish this. There's a huge difference between playing the part and actually being a visible leader—one who is accessible, approachable, and relatable. A visible leader is not a dispenser of information but a participant and dynamic facilitator of a true exchange of ideas between individuals and teams.

* * * *

The second component of trust-building is **transparency**, our willingness and ability to share information that matters, in plain and straightforward language. Doing so consistently is an act of trust in your people, just as hoarding or obscuring information communicates disregard for your people's welfare or relevance. Your choice in the matter—to share or withhold—will have a direct impact on their ability to trust you.

Transparency has many practical use cases. Share information, motives, and relevant decisions openly and honestly. Keep the team updated on what's going on both in the company and at the senior leadership level. Do not withhold resources from employees or make decisions in secret. Be clear about the team vision and expectations of team members. Practice open communication, as we discussed in chapter 5, keeping the "circuit" of information flowing to each member. Ask employees for their thoughts on workplace topics at regular check-in meetings. At all times, strive to create an environment where employees feel comfortable voicing their opinions—even if they differ from those in leadership.

Of course, transparency creates a high standard of accountability for a leader's own behavior. Rather than stick with comfortable routines, an "outside the boss" leader must constantly evaluate the effectiveness and strengths of her team—and of herself. Such a leader must send (and stand by) clear signals that she is worthy of trust. That includes searching for solutions, sincerely welcoming criticism, and taking responsibility for her part in the process, whatever happens. Doing this will allow the leader to set clear expectations and know that the team will understand and carry them out.

* * * *

Building trust also depends on an organization's (and its leaders') inherent *capability* to create a good work experience or environment. As we've mentioned earlier, this doesn't mean focusing on job perks or even financial compensation. Pay and benefits cannot be ignored, of course. However, they pale in comparison to the things that matter more.

TRUST REQUIRES A "COMMON DENOMINATOR," A SINGULAR VALUE THAT SUSTAINS THE WELL-BEING OF EVERY MEMBER.

In every endeavor requiring mutual trust, there must be a *common denominator*, a cause to strive for, a singular value that sustains the well-being of every member of the team. It can be about safety, quality, a sense of purpose or mission, personal security, or a combination of any of these. Such a common denominator provides a sense of belonging, fostering a sense of emotional investment and community. Of course, it must be based in reality, not empty words. Most importantly, it must be backed by the leader's and his organization's intention to get it right. Perks, however generous, can be like junk food—enjoyable in the moment but lacking the nutritional emotional value to sustain a healthy culture.

For my company, safety was paramount. Working on high-rise buildings meant that our team members had to work while suspended hundreds of feet above the ground! They also had to solve problems as they presented themselves, with minds free from worry about motors, cables, and harnesses. Theoretically, there were hundreds of moving parts, things that *could* go wrong, so the company's top priority was to ensure that they never did. Creating our safety-first work environment involved constant feedback from every member, testing every assumption, and being fully accountable at every level. Doing so proved our capability to everyone and served as a foundation for their loyalty and trust.

Proving such a capability, like every other component of trust, is a long-term commitment. However, leaders who prioritize the things their team values most will find that their team's trust will grow accordingly. It will make pay and benefits, however essential they may be, a secondary reason for staying with the team. It will also increase their engagement and satisfaction in ways that have a direct impact on the perceptions of our customers and partners.

* * * *

The final element in building a high-trust workplace is *reliability*. When a leader makes promises or commitments, he must back them up. Such credibility is the sole currency of business and the leader's character—as it is in life. The success or failure of any business depends on promises kept and value delivered, but that dynamic starts with the leader. If you talk it up, show up for it.

Being reliable doesn't mean being perfect, however. Inevitably, the best intentions are foiled by human error, miscalculation, or unforeseen events. This is why the first half of the book deals with vulnerability and clear communication.

> ## THE SECRET TO A LEADER'S RELIABILITY IS TO HAVE ONLY ONE VERSION OF HIMSELF.

To be clear, every leader needs to demonstrate and have confidence in his own expertise—just as he is confident in his team's expertise. But he must not pretend to be all-knowing. He must have the competent humility to seek answers to new or unforeseen problems. Whenever he faces challenges, he should be able to communicate about them openly. To be reliable is to be human in the best possible sense. The secret is for the leader to have only one version of himself, not an imaginary superhero and a hidden version that makes all the mistakes.

Another key to reliability is a leader's track record for fairness. Just as he should have only one version of himself and his abilities, a leader must also have one version of the requirements for being on the team. This applies especially to growth opportunities. No matter what their background or circumstances, all members should have the same access to learning experiences. Developing each member's skill sets can occur through training programs or special projects. It can also happen informally, through the leader's awareness of individual skills and potential—actively matching them to new opportunities that arise.

Reliability is not something you can fake. Employees and customers alike are good at detecting a false front, even if they don't have the words to describe it. But once a leader establishes the habit of consistently following through, trust invariably follows.

The High-Wire Act

There are many psychological reasons why people are drawn to extreme, inherently dangerous sports like BASE jumping or free climbing.[10] A similar vicarious thrill also attends the act of *watching* someone perform something dangerous, like the launch of a space shuttle, or something seemingly dangerous, like a performance by Cirque du Soleil. Movies and television abound with dangerous-looking events that boost our adrenaline and satisfy some primal feeling. But in reality, such things are less dangerous than they seem, because the main participant is never alone.

Earlier, we used the example of a parachute jumper. While technically alone during the event, the jumper is backed by an array of trusted partners, from the professionals who designed and built the equipment to those who provided instruction to the person who correctly packed the parachute. The same is true for other "solo" events. The BASE jumper and the free climber both have a network of unseen partners they must trust, since the main participant cannot possibly cover all aspects of the sport.

In the realm of fictional danger, the trust network is exponentially larger. A single stunt, especially one not created with CGI, involves weeks of planning, dozens of support staff and specialists, plus hours of careful rehearsal. The actor (or more likely the stunt double) knows and trusts her team of mostly unseen supporters. Ideally, each team member is vulnerable, open to adjustment, and communicating constantly. They trust that the stunt will come off as planned.

> **TRUST CAN AND OFTEN MUST BE IMPLICIT, BUT THERE CAN BE NO SHORTCUTS. REAL TRUST IS ALWAYS BASED ON EXPLICIT ACTIONS THAT WARRANT OUR TRUST.**

On occasion, however, that trust is misplaced, with tragic consequences. During filming of the movie *Rust*, cinematographer Halyna Hutchins was fatally shot because the prop gun used in a scene had been loaded with a live round. The movie's armorer was convicted of involuntary manslaughter, but the breakdown in trust went further than her. According to investigators, safety meetings were not conducted, and safety protocols were ignored. Before the shooting, an assistant director handled the gun himself instead of leaving it to the overworked and relatively inexperienced armorer. Trust can and often must be implicit, but there can be no shortcuts. Real trust is always based on explicit actions that warrant our trust. In the end, it was determined that the *Rust* production company's expedient practices undermined the practical basis for trust.

Outside movies and extreme sports, our reliance on trust is even more acute. Think about the launch of manned spacecraft since the early 1960s. Behind each thrilling and potentially dangerous event, a small army of experts must know their own limits, communicate constantly, and do everything possible to merit the trust of the few individuals sitting in the craft. Failures like the *Challenger* explosion are possible, as we saw in chapter 2. But every successful launch (and there have been over three hundred) has been characterized by trust.

Now, consider the less dramatic but equally risky endeavors your organization faces each day. Behind each action, there is a team of individuals, recognized or not, each of whom must be trusted to do their job well. But they cannot do their jobs well, or for long, if there isn't a practical basis for trust—their trust starts with you as the "switch" that keeps the circuit flowing.

You may often feel like a high-wire artist or a space shuttle pilot—alone and at the center of attention—but you are never truly alone. A team is behind you, but they can only perform at their best when they trust you as much as you must trust them. Taking the long journey through your humanity, your transparency, your proven capability, and your reliability will make that possible.

CHAPTER 9

HERE TO HELP

A relationship without trust is like a cell phone with no service; all you can do is play games.

—ANONYMOUS

A leader's trustworthiness cannot be measured in a scientific manner. That is the case for individual leaders like you and is certainly true for leaders as a group. Opinion surveys, even scientific ones, only confirm that people *prefer* to work in places where leaders can be trusted, communicate openly, and are open about their imperfections. They cannot give you a reliable "trustworthiness score" or show you how to become a more trusted leader.

There are of course *lagging* indicators of public trust—or the lack thereof. The former might include Alcoa. Its trajectory changed for the better under the leadership of Paul O'Neill, who gained enormous employee trust by prioritizing company safety.* On the other hand, a lack of trust is reflected in Boeing's recent stock price or in Volkswagen's sales numbers following the company's 2015 emissions scandal.

---

*You will read more about Paul O'Neill and Alcoa in a later chapter.

We can see a correlation between trust and the fate of a company or organization. But the fact is that *measuring* trust in an individual leader (especially yourself) is always *subjective*, even when the end results are observed. So, as we did in chapters 3 and 6, the answers must come from asking yourself questions.

QUESTIONS ABOUT TRUST

Ask yourself the following questions, and take time to consider the answers you would have given years ago, in your leadership position right now, and in the not-so-distant future:

- How often do you notice telltale signs of mistrust, including less feedback in meetings, increased absenteeism, and higher turnover?

- To what extent do members of your team express concerns about their own performance? How often do they ask for help?

- When you ask someone on your team to perform a task, is it something you would be willing to do yourself, if you could? Do they know that?

- Have you made it clear (by words *and* actions) that their safety, personal security, and well-being are your highest priorities?

- When interacting with members of your team, is there one "version" of who you are—

or does your persona change with the circumstances?

- To what extent do you take personal responsibility for outcomes, both positive and negative?

- To what extent do you expect others on your team to trust you implicitly, no matter what?

As with the questions in chapters 3 and 6, you cannot earn a numeric score on the issue of trust. However, thinking about these questions is an effective way to recalibrate your actions and, in time, begin to earn the trust that will make your organization successful.

To that end, let's consider three more hypothetical situations where trust is a major factor, and where it helps to "think outside the boss" as a true leader.

Money Matters

In 2009, Bernie Madoff pled guilty to multiple federal felony charges, including securities fraud, money laundering, and outright theft. Over a twenty-year period, he had defrauded his clients of nearly sixty-five billion dollars, in what was described as the largest investment Ponzi scheme in history.[1] More recently, hedge fund and tech entrepreneur Sam Bankman-Fried was convicted of criminal fraud and conspiracy, having funneled billions from investors in his cryptocurrency exchange, FTX.[2]

The Madoff and Bankman-Fried scandals share a common theme. Both men relied on the trust of multiple individuals—a trust based on misinformation and hubris—that they would benefit financially from being on the ground floor of a "sure thing." The misplaced trust was based not only on personal bias (*He seems like a really smart guy*) but also on some level of ignorance (*I don't understand this stuff, but it sounds like a great idea*).

To compound matters, the *personal* trust element they violated was compounded by their victim's trust in a *situation*. For Madoff, it was complex securities; for Bankman-Fried, it was the mysterious realm of unregulated cryptocurrency.* Not only did these criminals rely on people's trust in their motives, but they also convinced their victims to trust in their expertise.

In one sense, financial investment *does* require specialized expertise. Investments by individuals who engage in active trading significantly underperform those involving market-based funds, such as those based on the S&P 500.[3] In another sense, however, mere mortals can understand the basic principles, even if it takes an experienced professional to handle them. Like Warren Buffett, wise investors should invest in businesses, not stocks. Investing in a company (or a group of companies) with proven strengths, and holding on for the long term, is vastly better than reacting to short-term stock price fluctuations.[4]

BUILDING TRUST IS THE WORK OF A LIFETIME. IT'S NOT A ROTE, ONCE-AND-DONE FORMULA.

Which brings us to our next exercise—a hypothetical financial services company. Imagine yourself as a leader in such an agency. For the sake of this exercise, let's assume that your company is

---

*Crypto is based on a perfectly valid technology, blockchain, as are other alleged commodities like NFTs. The fault is not a problem with the technology itself, which is quite promising, but with our trust in someone's word that the item in question has intrinsic value.

acting as a *fiduciary*, one who is legally and ethically required to act solely in the best interests of the client. On a daily basis, you are handling your clients' wealth, charged with increasing its value, keeping it secure for the future, or most likely both. As a leader, consider how trust can be advanced in the following situations:

- Bona fide fiduciaries often acquire new accounts of individuals who have worked with more traditional, high-commission stock brokerages. How would you demonstrate the difference to a new client? In what ways can you actively listen to and empathize with their personal aspirations and fears when it comes to money?

- We are bombarded with worldwide financial news, from inflation to trade and the doings of huge corporations. How will your financial advice be different from the firehose of information they experience every day?

- Your hypothetical company has several partners and associates serving clients. How can you earn their trust and lead them by example, without breaching client confidentiality about specific investments?

- Like any other business, financial services companies make mistakes, sometimes costly ones. How would you handle such a mistake involving a client's portfolio? How would you handle a mistake affecting the well-being of your partners or associates?

- In what ways are your successful actions dependent on other individuals in the company? In what ways are their successes dependent on you? How would you recognize and support the person or persons who "packed your parachute," so to speak?

Building trust requires both personal vulnerability—not assuming you're always right—and constant, open communication, as we covered in the first half of the book. None of these things happen overnight; they take time. Simply put, building trust and maintaining it is the work of a lifetime. It's not a rote, once-and-done formula.

All the News That Fits

Our first hypothetical situation included the fact that today we are bombarded with information during almost every waking moment. It's a curve that began with radio and television and increased exponentially in the 1970s (with the invention of email) and early 1990s (the web). It has skyrocketed ever since, as smartphones have increasingly become our internet IEDs.[*]

Leaving the social and psychological implications of this curve aside, one thing is clear: the news media business will never be the same. As advertising and subscription models are disrupted daily, media companies struggle to pay reporters—not to mention the editors and fact-checkers who make sure stories are accurate and engaging. Anyone with an opinion can be read or viewed by anyone with a smartphone. This undermines the viability of news reporting—through the sheer volume of noise posing as information.

The results are concerning. With more competition for our attention and fewer resources to devote to actual reporting, people's trust in the news is at an all-time low.[†] Politics in particular is a "trust desert" for media outlets, with only 14 percent of those surveyed in a recent poll expressing a great deal of confidence in

---

[*]Instant Entertainment Devices
[†]To be fair, the credibility of news reporting has always had its ups and downs, but historically, the choices were clearer—between reputable newspapers and the tabloids, for example—when the media choices were fewer.

election-related information received from national sources.[5] People are also understandably concerned about news generated by AI or by entities or governments peddling deliberate misinformation.

With all those problems in mind, imagine yourself at the head of a hypothetical media organization, if you dare. For the sake of the discussion, let's imagine it as a local news entity, with both print and online media in its channel portfolio. Since the lifeblood of such entities is its credibility with the public, consider the following in the framework of establishing trust:

- Your reporters' coverage frequently mentions people and companies connected to your regular advertisers, directly or indirectly. How do you guide your reporters in dealing with this potential conflict of interest? How and when do you tell your advertisers about a story affecting them?

- How does your organization report on controversial social or political topics? Knowing that some people will be offended by such stories, how does your organization maintain its objectivity? How do you convey that objectivity without compromising source confidentiality?

- Reporters can make mistakes, and these days, such errors are revealed to the public more quickly than ever. What is the first thing you and your organization do when a mistake is made? To whom should a mistake be acknowledged, and should you take personal responsibility?

- When a team member struggles with an assignment, are you willing to step in and assist, without taking undue credit?

- When a reporter faces public criticism, justified or not,

are you willing to defend him and his reputation, even at the risk of your own?

If the last question reminds you of the Ben Bradlee character in the film *All the President's Men*, it was intended to. At the time of Watergate, *The Washington Post* was basically a local paper. In real life as in the movie, Bradlee earned the trust of his reporters, and of his readers, by standing up for his people and his principles, regardless of the fallout.

Passing the Ball

Prior to the 1991 NBA finals, superstar Michael Jordan was not well known for his trust in other players. After all, he had averaged over thirty points per game since the 1986-87 season, on his way to becoming one of the league's all-time top scorers. His undoubted scoring prowess had led to the unspoken belief that he could carry the team by himself.[6] But in the 1991 series, something changed, highlighting the first of many NBA championships for the Chicago Bulls.

During the decisive final game, the Los Angeles Lakers were putting enormous and understandable defensive pressure on Jordan. In the final quarter, head coach Phil Jackson told Jordan to start passing to guard John Paxson, who had averaged only 8.7 points per game during the season. Jordan did, and Paxson's last-minute scoring surge clinched the title.

Jordan's trust in his fellow players was not a one-time event. In the nail-biting finale of the 1993 championship series, he had scored all of the Bulls' fourth-quarter points. But with seconds remaining, and Jordan expected to make the dramatic final score, the ball—and the winning shot—went to Paxson.

For our final hypothetical scenario, you'll need to imagine yourself as a player, or perhaps a player-coach, on an organized sports team. For this exercise, assume that you have proven athletic skill and experience. (Even if you don't, I'm sure you've entertained the thought.) Whatever the reality may be, consider how you'd act in the following circumstances:

- During a practice session, a player you're defending against makes a gain or scores a point against your side. How do you celebrate that (without being condescending)?

- During a game, a player with less experience and skill than you signals for the ball. What is your first thought?

- After a win (and after a loss), whom do you usually credit (or blame) for the outcome?

- Assume you are a "seasoned" and highly successful player with a great store of experience and skills. How (and how much) do you share that information with other players?

- When a player is having prolonged difficulty with some aspect of the game, what do you do?

- When you are having similar difficulties, what are others likely to do?

It is easy for many of us to fancy ourselves in heroic sports scenarios. So, if you can, be as realistic as possible. Better still, reimagine the sports example as a metaphor for your less glamorous role as a business leader. As a proactive player-coach, what can you do to make each player feel a part of winning the game?

✳ ✳ ✳ ✳

Trust is not limited to these three hypotheticals, of course. Every business and nonprofit on the planet depends on the trust of others to do what they promised to do, to prove their intrinsic value. That trust, the wellspring of an organization's success, is powered solely by the trust its leaders and team members have in one another. It happens when leaders weave implicit trust into the fabric of the organization, through a consistent series of explicit trust-building actions. By building that connection, the stage is set for the final piece of the leadership puzzle: a shared clarity of mission.

PART IV

MISSION

CHAPTER 10

THE IMPORTANCE OF MISSION

You can't see what you don't understand.
But what you think you already understand,
you'll fail to notice.

—RICHARD POWERS

For many special-purpose teams of people, a singular mission is essential. These range from military units to field-based charities to aid and rescue operations. Their missions tend to be straight-forward, as are the strategies to perform their missions well. For a military team, it's a version of "take (or hold) that piece of territory." For field charities like World Central Kitchen, it's "feed X-number of people." For aid and rescue teams like the Red Cross, it's setting up emergency shelters and medical facilities after a disaster. But for leaders running ordinary businesses, the nature of their mission is more complex.

First, mission begins to define the company's purpose and direction. While a written *statement* of that mission is not always effective in doing that (see the next page), the mission itself is not the words alone. It involves concrete goals that are understood and pursued by everyone. Knowing the company's ultimate direction guides in strategic decision-making and can differentiate the company from its competitors. It can also inspire and motivate team members to perform at their best, provided they are personally vested with the same mission.

One thing is certain, however. A valid organizational mission is *not* about making more money. Profitability and efficiency are the *byproducts* of a sound and clearly understood mission, not its root causes. When a mission transcends the words used to describe it, and when it is clearly understood and embraced by the entire group, it has the power to drive success on many levels.

Mission Misstatements

A lot of ink and pixels have been spent describing the value (or the problem) of having a written mission or vision *statement* for your organization. The problem is that the two words (mission and vision) are not even the same thing, nor do they encompass every possible business strategy.[1] But more important is the fact that, no matter what you call them or how they relate to your actual strategy, these high-sounding words simply don't do what we think they should.[2]

For one thing, formal mission statements are often generic marketing slogans that make your organization sound exactly like every other. It's as if the statement were written by artificial intelligence, which some of them may be.

MARKETING-SPEAK

To illustrate the bland, generic, and largely meaningless nature of many mission statements, here's an example of one created literally, and in a matter of seconds, by an AI-powered mission statement generator. The only prompts were the company name ("XYZCompany"), what the company does ("We make the best widgets in the world"), and the desired tone ("compelling"). The results were thematically correct but lacked meaningful substance:

> *Empowering Innovation, One Widget at a Time.*
>
> *"At XYZCompany, we're driven by a passion to create exceptional widgets that exceed our customers' expectations and inspire a world of possibility. We're committed to pushing the boundaries of innovation, quality, and customer satisfaction, fueled by a relentless pursuit of excellence and a dedication to making a meaningful impact.*

> *"Our mission is to design, manufacture, and deliver the most exceptional widgets on the planet, empowering our customers to achieve their goals, dreams, and aspirations. We strive to create a culture of innovation, collaboration, and continuous improvement, where our team members can grow, thrive, and make a difference.*
>
> *"Together, we're shaping a brighter future, one widget at a time."*

You can be forgiven for not taking the above example seriously, or for glossing over the clichéd, hyperbolic language.* But the truth is that many of us are content with nice-sounding words created for outside consumption but divorced from the reality of what the organization does well, and from its shared principles. In other words, having a mission *statement* is entirely different from having a mission or purpose—one that is shared throughout the organization.

What IS Your Mission?

Let's start by describing what mission is ***not***. These days, we're likely to think of our mission in emotional, even fantastic, terms, as if we live in the Marvel Universe or serve some higher power intent on saving humanity. But even in the toned-down version of that idea, what we think of as our mission, mistakenly, is

---

* To be fair, the site I used for this example recommends that humans edit the results "to achieve the perfect tone and messaging," but chances are that the results will still be generic and forgettable. Part of the problem is the nature of AI itself, which uses words written by humans asits training data. If those humans write in empty clichés, AI will follow suit.

more about subjective feelings than about reality. Unfortunately, when we think of a mission in purely emotional terms, perhaps as part of a marketing message, the actual substance is left behind.

Part of an organization's mission is about what it *does*, but it's a mistake to think yours is the only one that does it well. Chances are good that, even if you are striving to be the best at something, you'll have plenty of company. And, as we saw while discussing humility, there will always be things you don't know and have yet to learn—even where you're an expert.

Also, a true mission is never the product of a charismatic or popular leader's thoughts, no matter how insightful they may seem. Not only does that run counter to the ideals of competent humility, communication, and trust, but assigning the word "mission" to one leader's persona will always fail in the long run. Witness the rise and fall of celebrity CEOs like Dennis Kozlowski and Elizabeth Holmes, and of the businesses they once so tightly controlled.

AN ORGANIZATION'S MISSION IS ABOUT THE COMBINED GOALS AND ASPIRATIONS OF ITS MEMBERS.

While a good leader does have a lot to say about an organization's mission, it is much more about the combined goals and aspirations of its members—the people who make things happen. The leader's job is to make the connections, to throw the switch and complete the circuit, as it were. Knowing what her teams are capable of—and putting them in the best place to do it—establishes a true sense of mission in each individual in ways that words can barely describe.

* * * *

In my experience, there is a powerful connection between mission and all the people who embody and fulfill it. Some will do so to a greater or lesser extent, of course. Not all individuals can achieve that clarity, however, despite the leader's intentions. Some fall short, or even fail spectacularly, while others excel.

The leader's challenge, then, is not only to connect individuals with their part in the overall mission but also to know that some will succeed far more than others, as the following account demonstrates. In spite of this, it is always the leader's responsibility to discover the goals and aspirations of individual team members—and to find ways to include them in the team's larger purpose. One especially vivid example illustrates this.

In 1995, a natural disaster struck the home of a boy named Francisco, someone who would later become part of my company's success. That year, the Category 5 Hurricane Mitch tore through Central America, claiming over 11,000 lives, including most of Francisco's family. Their home was obliterated in moments by a flood that swept through their village, leaving only Francisco hanging on to a piece of roof, and his brother Jamie, miles downriver, separated but miraculously alive.

Eventually, both boys moved to the United States. After the disaster, Francisco had vowed never to let anything stop him from doing something meaningful with his life. So, in 2004, at age eighteen, instead of going to college, he decided to learn a trade, starting as a laborer with my company. His work ethic and his hunger for knowledge were apparent right away, so I assigned him to a mentor and started providing the training he needed. He wanted to learn English, and how to read blueprints, so I helped place him in school and reimbursed him. He was paired with skilled technicians to improve his skills and further his development.

Francisco's brother Jamie took a different road. He was exposed to similar opportunities but started drinking and eventually ended up in a losing struggle with addiction. He was deported after several brushes with the law. He lacked his brother's personal clarity of mission, and in the end was unable to find clarity anywhere else. Today, however, Francisco's focus on his personal mission—one that coincided with mine—is a root cause of his success. As I began the process of divesting from my business, he was well on track to creating one of his own.

> ## UNDERSTANDING EMPLOYEES AND THEIR GOALS IS THE MOST CONSTRUCTIVE THING A LEADER CAN DO TO BECOME A BETTER LEADER.

Mutual clarity of mission is *not* about generating warm feelings. It's also not about sacrificing any of the leader's interests for the sake of his people. Understanding employees and their personal goals is the most constructive thing a leader can do to become a better leader. Giving them the tools to do their job is the most effective way to build them up, and to equip them to help achieve their goals, and by default the company's goals as well.

Meaning and Purpose

Think of mission as having a central core, the things that are crucial to the success or even the survival of a business. On the surface, this must include financial realities—whether enough revenue can be made to meet or exceed the costs of operating. It also must include providing *something*, a product or a service that human beings need or want—the reason they're willing to pay you instead of doing it themselves.

This is an extremely simplified view; economists have far more complicated explanations.[3] But what they often overlook is that an organization's mission or goal is inextricably entwined with that of its people. If the organization's mission is at odds with theirs, at any level, then no amount of money or perks will be enough to keep things moving in the right direction.

Think about mission as having three distinct layers, each one involving your company, your employees, their goals and aspirations—all that is meaningful to them personally. When the organization's mission and theirs coincide at all three levels, then you will be building a sustainably successful business.

Positive Future for
Family, Community, and Beyond

OUTSIDE OUR WORK

WITH OUR CUSTOMERS

Outstanding
Customer Experience

WITHIN OUR ORGANIZATION

Safe and
Constructive Work
Environment
Where Employees
Can Thrive
and Grow

Builds a
Company
That Will
Thrive

The inner core of this mission are the things a company and its leaders can control or influence directly. In essence, that part of the mission is *to provide a safe and constructive work environment where employees can thrive and achieve excellence.* This includes basics like compensation and benefits, as well as policies and practices affecting safety, efficiency, and your employees' opportunity to improve and enhance their skills and position. It also includes less tangible but vital elements such as company culture and fair policies for employment and review. But what the company controls is only a part of what employees deem essential. The work they do for the organization and their identification with its mission must be meaningful to *them.*

The next layer includes the many ways in which employees work with customers, clients, and strategic partners, both individually and in teams. In essence, that part of the mission is *to deliver a remarkable customer experience, one that actively serves the client's best interests.* There are lots of companies that promise exceptional service but relatively few that deliver as if they had a vested interest in the customer's success.

It is at this level that leadership often fails to enable their people to understand, see, and carry out the mission. Whether out of a lack of true humility, out of poor communication, or due to a lack of trust, they assume an "I'm-the-boss-so-do-as-I say" attitude, making the paycheck and benefits the only reason for employees to work with customers. But people outside the company can always detect those who are disengaged, just in it for the paycheck and waiting for the clock to tick away until it's time to clock out. They can see that the only "mission" at work is purely transactional, and they are disinclined to work closely with the company.

> **WHEN EMPLOYEES ARE INVESTED IN CUSTOMER SATISFACTION AND ARE EMPOWERED TO MAKE DECISIONS, THEIR SENSE OF PURPOSE AND MEANING WILL INEVITABLY LINE UP WITH YOURS.**

The opposite is true when those same employees are invested in their customers' outcomes, and are given the means to make intelligent, autonomous decisions. Then their sense of purpose and meaning intersects beautifully with that of your company. Customers and strategic partners will pick up this vibe immediately and respond in kind. When employees know that they have the support of trusted (and imperfect) colleagues who know how to communicate and support one another, everyone is empowered to excel.

Beyond the inner workings of the organization, and beyond the work your people do with customers, is the visible layer of a leader's mission—the personal aspirations and goals of your individual employees. Usually, these are things they do outside work, for themselves, for family and friends, and for people they care about in general. In essence, the focus of this part of the mission is *to create impact beyond our work by fostering a humane work experience for employees while also impacting their communities.*

This doesn't have to be complicated. All human beings desire "life, liberty, and the pursuit of happiness." It can be as simple as providing security and a future for their children, or as complicated as a cause or belief. But unless the leader takes time to know what his employees aspire to *specifically*, to the greatest extent possible, he will lack the understanding to incorporate their purpose into the whole.

> **WHEN YOU KNOW WHAT MOTIVATES YOUR PEOPLE, THE DOOR IS OPEN TO MATCH THEM WITH OPPORTUNITIES THAT BENEFIT THEM AS WELL AS THE ORGANIZATION.**

It is never a leader's job to dictate *how* these goals must be fulfilled. However, it is always a good idea for a leader to know and understand what his colleagues care about and where they want to go, and to empower them with the resources to get there. It is a long process, to be undertaken with the greatest care and respect. And when you come to know what motivates and moves your people, the door is wide open to match them with opportunities that benefit them as well as the organization.

Whether the mission focus is inside the company, in relationship with customers, or outside of everyday work responsibilities, a leader's primary responsibility is to know how it relates to employees' real needs—and to be sure *they* know it too.

Seeing the Bigger Picture

Sometimes, a high-profile event illustrates the importance of a singular, clearly understood mission. It can also reveal the elements of the mission that are not always understood at first. Such an event occurred in the summer of 2018: the successful Tham Luang cave rescue operation in northern Thailand.

At the time, the drama captured world attention, and has since become the subject of documentaries, books, and films. Twelve teenage and preteen soccer players and their assistant coach were trapped deep inside the caves, as early monsoon rains filled the cave network and blocked their way out. After a long and perilous search, the group was found. Eventually, each boy had to be sedated as they were individually carried through the underwater network, wearing wetsuits and oxygen masks—a journey that lasted three hours each. During the eighteen-day operation, one Thai Navy SEAL diver was killed and another died from an infection incurred during the rescue, but in the end, all thirteen boys and their coach were saved.

The overall mission was obvious, although considered impossible at first. Thai divers were impeded by heavy rains and rising floodwaters, prompting ongoing efforts to pump millions of gallons out of the caves. Once the boys and their coach were located, many options were proposed and rejected, including finding or drilling an alternate route or just waiting until the end of the monsoon season and supplying them with food, water, oxygen, and a phone connection. But in the end, the only alternative, however dangerous, was the diving option.

Teams and experts from nineteen countries contributed to solving a myriad of complex challenges, all leading to the largely successful outcome. Officials also had to deal with mounting public pressure and criticism, both during and after the event. The boys themselves were subject to intense media attention afterward, and the coach was criticized (but then exonerated) for taking unnecessary risks.

The dynamics of everyone's clarity of mission were impressive, and the results went well beyond the saving of thirteen lives. Team members who had never worked together managed to communicate new findings and make mutual adjustments to their plans. Each person understood and embraced the overall mission—creating individual, task-specific missions that meshed with the whole. Even after the successful rescue, the boys' ability to cope with unwanted public attention was supported by Thai officials, who took steps to ensure that they thrived after the experience. In other words, the mission transcended their mere survival, and became a means for pursuing their own aspirations.[4]

* * * *

When leaders prioritize aspects of their companies' mission that mesh with the needs of their people, great things happen for the company. But these benefits can get lost when the rhetoric is not genuine. Here are some well-worn examples. Each can burnish a company's PR profile, but they are only effective when the mission objective is a truly shared one—and is clear in everyone's minds:

Wellness has become an overused term these days. First coined in the 1950s (combining "well-being" and "fitness"), the word meant not just the absence of illness but the ability to thrive physically and mentally. This is a good thing, of course, but it requires some examination before it can be part of the mission.

The global wellness market today is believed to be worth over 1.5 trillion dollars.[5] But because the term is not well defined, it has often been used as a marketing tactic. Products and services sold this way may not be effective or safe. Companies may also offer superficial "wellness programs" as a perk while also ignoring deeper workplace problems.

Actual wellness, on the other hand, is something that every employee desires—for themselves, their coworkers, and especially their families. Part of the leader's mission, then, is to acknowledge that fact, to understand that it may be different for each person, and to communicate that you know its importance. A leader also needs to "walk the talk." Meditation classes are not a bad thing, but a decent health insurance plan is better.

Safety is obviously critical in construction and in similar businesses, but it is part of any workplace environment—even when we work from home. The National Association of Safety Professionals lists workplace hazards that include the ergonomic and psychological as well as the structural and environmental.[6] But when companies deal with safety mainly as a compliance issue, or to reduce their potential legal liability, they are missing a key aspect of clarity of mission.

Everyone wants to be safe from harm. Without the persistent fear that something bad may happen, we are free to excel at our roles—which in turn benefits the company as a whole. Research has shown that there's a connection between a healthy workplace, employee well-being, and good organizational outcomes—but only if there is effective communication and alignment within the organization.[7]

Leaders have an important role here. It is not enough to post safety rules or hold occasional government-mandated safety classes. To make safety a real part of the mission, a leader must listen to his people, and not assume he has all the answers. Communication must go both ways, and he must continue to do what is necessary to ensure a high level of trust. Knowing that they have a say, and that their safety is a high priority, is a clear communication of a common mission—one that ensures engagement and financial success.

Career advancement opportunity is the third example of a common mission objective, but unfortunately, many leaders give only lip service to the idea. In practice, they prioritize short-term profitability over their employees' future. They may be too busy to bother, or feel threatened by others' potential, or they simply may not care. This always leads to a lack of transparency, forcing employees to seek advancement on their own.[8]

The danger is that employees are likely to seek advancement outside their current company, at enormous cost in turnover and retraining. But simply having an internal career advancement track is not sufficient, especially if the only incentive is a bigger paycheck.

A leader with clarity of mission has an advantage when it comes to career advancement. First of all, if he actually knows his people, he will be able to match their capabilities with opportunities to learn and handle new situations. Without question, this requires the leader to remain vulnerable—to not be the know-it-all boss and to admit that others have knowledge he may not. It requires constant two-way communication. And it demands that the leader earn their trust by taking responsibility and being willing to do the things he requires of others. When he does, others will pick up that same clarity of mission and adopt it as their own.

The True Bottom Line

In a recent McKinsey survey, almost two-thirds of US–based employees said that COVID-19 had caused them to reflect on their purpose in life, with nearly half saying they were reconsidering the kind of work they do.[9] The same survey found that *70 percent said their sense of purpose is defined by their work.* This is both a challenge and an opportunity.

Put together, these findings spell trouble for companies that ignore their employees' individual goals and aspirations. But when leaders take the time to make the mission clear to everyone—at every level of activity—and discover what each person truly needs, they empower their people and align their desires and goals with those of the organization.

* * * *

One of the great barriers to shared clarity of mission is the often-mundane nature of work. Not everyone can be an astronaut or a rock star or a driver in the Grand Prix. Most of us have normal, everyday jobs, filled with routine tasks like cleaning, maintaining equipment, making deliveries, and writing reports. In my own company, there were exciting parts of the job, like rappelling down the outside of a multistory building, networking, and meeting new clients, but there were plenty of boring tasks to go around.

> ## NO MATTER HOW MUNDANE OR INSIGNIFICANT A TASK MAY SEEM, OR HOW SMALL A PERSON'S ROLE MAY APPEAR TO THE UNTRAINED EYE, THEY ALL CAN LEAD TO SUCCESS.

But despite appearances, even the most boring task is an essential piece of a company's overall mission. The work of a custodian at NASA or at a hospital may not make headlines, but that doesn't mean he isn't an integral part of the team. Likewise, new or inexperienced team members are just as likely as veterans to detect a problem or come up with a solution—*if* they clearly see the mission and have a vested interest in its outcome.

So-called ordinary tasks are a part of every level of the mission, from within the company's internal processes to its interactions with others. They also occupy our daily lives outside work. Life is filled with ordinary, everyday events that would get almost no "likes" or "upvotes" on social media. But they are still part of what gives our lives meaning and purpose. It is the leader's job not only to know what those tasks are, and who does them, but also to know why they matter—and to let the employees know that every day, in actions as well as words.

Employee-centric clarity of mission produces measurable results. When employees know that their needs and the company's needs are aligned, two things happen. First, they are far less likely to leave—even for a bigger paycheck or more perks. Belonging to an organization that considers them members, not commodities, ensures their longevity, avoiding the huge cost of recruiting and training their replacements. Second, all members are highly motivated to improve performance and seek new opportunities within their own sphere.

No matter how ordinary or insignificant a task may seem, or how small a person's role may appear to the untrained eye, they all can lead to success. If the mission is clear and mutual, success is assured.

CHAPTER 11

SEEING AROUND THE CORNER

Leadership is having a vision:
What's my goal? Then, part two is getting to
know the people who are working with me, and
what their goals are. And then the real definition
of leadership is making those two merge.

—MARK CUBAN

When we learn to walk, ride a bike, drive a car, or anything else that takes us from Point A to Point B, the early learning part is unsteady at best. Toddlers go through several stages before taking their first steps. They are tentative at first, looking immediately ahead and taking deliberate steps one at a time. But when they have a definite objective in sight—like an encouraging parent—walking becomes surer and more natural. Soon, no unlocked space is out of bounds.

Learning to use a bike or drive a car is similar. Beginners wobble or swerve as they look immediately ahead and over-think every move. Once the mechanical actions become habitual, however, and especially when we're thinking of **and looking for** the destination, the car seems to "drive itself."

In the early days of auto racing, you could observe what the driver was looking at. It was seldom the track in front of him; he was aware of cars around him, but his attention was on the next curve and beyond. The same is true of competitive motorcycling today. Look at photos of motorcycle racers rounding a curve. They are not looking straight ahead; they're looking to see what's around the corner.

Clarity of mission is all about that. When you and your people are narrowly focused on what's ahead, you will wobble and fall more often than not. But when you know your people and help them see around the corner—beyond the transactional—then it's game on, and the big race can be won.

* * * *

I have always been fascinated—some have called it obsessed—with fast, powerful cars. I grew up watching the likes of Mario Andretti, Emerson Fittipaldi, and Niki Lauda. I remember wondering, *how can you make something that powerful work for you? How is it possible to work with that, when decisions must be made in an instant—or what seemed like even less time than that?*

When my heroes weren't racing, they gave countless interviews, which I devoured. It was never about how much power was in their Formula One beauties, or how fast they could go. It was always about the driver's skill, his instinct about what lay ahead, and about practice, practice, practice.

The first car I owned was powerful, even by today's standards. So, from the first time I took the wheel, I was hooked. But I didn't have the skills to drive it the way it was meant to be driven. After a couple of close calls, I knew I had to find out what my idols meant in all those interviews. Even if I never raced professionally, I knew I had to learn how to handle all that power safely.

So, I started paying attention, trying to figure out how to do things safely. I decided to train at BMW's performance center in Spartanburg, South Carolina, but before I managed to go, BMW held a special event on a track built in the enormous parking lot of DC's RFK Stadium and invited the public to come and try their high-performance cars. I jumped at the chance, signed up, and was hooked all over again.

But in my first try with a real racing machine, I learned how far out of my league I really was. At first, I was hesitating and over-steering constantly, reacting to whatever I saw directly in front of the car. I was like a seventeen-year-old trying to make a left turn in Driver's Ed class. I'm sure I made the instructor's adrenaline spike. Mine was definitely up but not in a fun way. While taking curves at high speed, I left the track several times and hugged the shoulder big time, prompting him to shout his instructions—to correct my direction and my pressure on the gas pedal. It was a rough morning.

During the midday break, he said something that seemed straight out of the Captain Obvious playbook. "The car will only go where you tell it to go." Then he explained, "In order to do that, lock your eyes on the exact spot where you want to go." It was my breakthrough. When I tried it, it was the beginning of an experience with these vehicles that was actually *fun*. I later furthered my training on a professional course. But these experiences also gave me some massive life and leadership lessons that went beyond the racetrack.

* * * *

As a leader, you can be *in* the moment but must not be swayed *by* the moment. Don't react to what is happening immediately in front of you—jerking the wheel back and forth and going off the track, as it were. Your responsibility is to know and understand who you are, what you're doing, and why you are doing it. Above all, it is about *where you are going* and how you intend to get there. If those things are not clear in your mind, they certainly won't be clear for your team. But the more your team can "see around the corner" with you, the more effectively you will stay on track and the faster you will be able to go.

> ONCE A LEADER UNDERSTANDS HIS PEOPLE'S GOALS, AND DISCOVERS WHERE THEIR GOALS AND HIS INTERSECT, STEERING THROUGH OBSTACLES AND DIFFICULTIES BECOMES SECOND NATURE.

If you want to engage other people on your journey, your clarity of mission and theirs must be mutual. The place you want to go and the place they want to go cannot be two separate, disconnected things. It's not a case of forcing them to see and do things your way; it is about fostering creativity; it's about knowing your people and their goals, and about finding the sweet spot where their goals and yours intersect. Once you see that clearly, steering through obstacles and difficulties becomes second nature—even at high speeds.

Things That Get in the Way

Unfortunately, the opposite is true for many organizations. Have you ever been involved with a project where you believed everyone involved was on the same page, working toward a goal that was clear to you, only to have everything come apart? Without warning, everyone has left the track, and there is a pileup on the curb, so to speak, all pulling in separate directions. Clearly, your view of the mission and how to get there was not theirs. But the temptation for many leaders today is to respond in the moment, pulling hard to bring things back on track but only managing to swerve and lose control. In the struggle, they lose sight of the goal, as does everyone else. In far too many cases, companies repeat the same pattern over and over again and struggle to master each successive challenge.

There are early warning signs of an organization's lack of clarity, even before it results in a crisis. One is the prevalence of *mixed messages*. It can be obvious, as when a leader says one thing but is clearly expecting something else (or worse, *doing* something that obviously contradicts his statements). It can also be more subtle, as when a leader hides behind jargon and meaningless catch phrases—either because he doesn't know what needs to be done or because he lacks the interest. In either case, the net result is constant confusion.

Another warning sign is a general *absence of accountability*. Whether it's a missed deadline, poor quality work, or a casually broken promise, the "not my job" mentality is a sure sign that team members are not sharing the same mission—much less seeing a goal that's just around the corner.

The other signs are all too common. Constant *frustration and friction* among coworkers are seldom caused by the difficulty of a task. They are nearly always signs that the team doesn't see where they're going and are convinced their leaders don't see it or even care if they get there. Needless to say, the end result of constantly swerving in and out of control is systemic low productivity, low morale, and fragmentation throughout the organization.

> **ACHIEVING CLARITY OF MISSION IS A QUALITY OF LEADERSHIP THAT BUILDS UP YOUR PEOPLE—EMPOWERING AND ENABLING THEM TO BUILD YOUR COMPANY.**

Without clarity of mission, the resulting internal disarray always rears its ugly head in financial losses and eats away at whatever motivation people may have had at the beginning. The tragedy is that so many businesses have accepted this level of dysfunction and considered it business as usual. In a way, it's a self-fulfilling prophecy. As much as they want their powerful organization to succeed, their inability to see what's around the corner—for their entire team—only results in careening back and forth, sowing more confusion and further clouding their sight.

However, this does not have to be the case. Achieving clarity of mission, as with vulnerability, communication, and trust, is a quality of leadership that *builds up your people*—empowering and enabling them to build your company.

The Building Blocks

Clarity of mission is not a crude, transactional process. It is foundational and organic. No number of perks, pep rallies, or motivational posters will replace the time and effort required to develop that clarity and make it a shared value. Rather, it can only be accomplished by practicing the fundamentals.

Those fundamentals boil down to the character of the leader, and to his willingness to build up his people, so they can build the business.

> ## A GOOD LEADER KNOWS THE LONG-TERM MISSION BUT DOES NOT SEE HIMSELF AS ITS INFALLIBLE SOURCE.

To achieve clarity of mission, a leader must practice the principles described earlier in the book, beginning with *vulnerability*. A leader should know his company's long-term mission, and be competent to lead others in that mission, but he cannot see himself as its infallible source. The reality is that the mission sometimes evolves from its original form. A vulnerable leader must have both the competence and the humility to recognize the insights that others may have in its evolution—to improve or even reshape the mission.

Vulnerability and clarity of mission are always complementary.[1] Being open about one's weaknesses and mistakes signals self-awareness and emotional intelligence, inviting a similar response from others. This invites different perspectives and insights, both to fulfill the long-term goal and to modify it when necessary. This joint approach, made possible only by the leader's humility, aligns the entire group with its now *shared* goals and priorities, reducing ambiguity and motivating others to bring their "A" game.

COMMUNICATING CLARITY OF MISSION MUST BE A TWO-WAY DIALOGUE, RESPONSIVE TO CHANGING CONTEXT AND NEEDS.

The second essential building block is of course *communication*. As we saw earlier, this does not mean hierarchical, top-down proclamation. Studies show that codified statements of company mission and organizational values are simply not enough.[2] Employees should take the meaning of the mission and its values personally and exercise them passionately. Communicating clarity of mission must also be *a two-way dialogue*, ensuring that it remains dynamic and responsive to changing context and needs. It must also include celebration—making it known when team members have excelled in meeting the goal, or even adjusting it when the need arises.

Of course, good communication does not always have to be profound or life-changing. On everyday matters, a good leader simply needs to be clear and consistent when assigning tasks. People often just need to have realistic, attainable goals and clear timelines. They may never change the course of the company—or even want to—but they'll know they're being respected and valued for their work.

Finally, to have a strong, mutually held clarity of mission, a leader must cultivate a climate of *trust*. As we saw, that must begin with the leader showing trust in others. Like the leaders, divers, and specialists at the Tham Luang cave rescue, each member must trust in the expertise of other team members and continue to give them good cause to return that trust.

Leading by Example

The most effective way to give every employee a true sense of ownership in the company mission is for you to demonstrate your own stake in the outcome. That means being willing to *do* the things you ask of them, not merely tell them what to do. This is not to show off or curry favor. You do this to communicate the significance of the work and, most importantly, to affirm *their* value to the organization and its mission. By being willing to lead by example, *the leader personifies the mission*.

That's a lot to take in. Obviously, a leader can't do everything; that's why the organization has employees! Nor should she be filling in or compensating for any deficits in other team members' responsibilities. If they are not doing their jobs, the company has bigger problems. But when a project requires an "all hands" response, a leader should provide two of those hands.

Working "in the trenches" is not always possible, of course, but there are other ways to lead by example. The most important is *showing others your real self*, not hiding behind a "boss" persona—or behind a literal office door. This is tricky when the organization is a large one, but it is absolutely essential. Clarity of mission requires clarity of identity. A true leader will take every opportunity to define who she truly is, in both words and actions.

* * * *

In the mid-1980s, I knew of an architecture student at an extremely competitive Ivy League university. Like most students, he had a grueling workload, made impossible by a sudden financial crisis. As a last resort, he made an appointment to see the dean of the college—someone he had never met in person.

At the meeting, he nervously explained that his scholarship

funds had run out, and that his financial situation would not allow him to continue. The dean listened and pointed him to several possible resources and options. But as the conversation went on, the dean asked an unexpected question.

Noticing that the student was wearing a religious emblem, the dean asked, "Have you tried praying about it?" The student was taken aback; he realized that he hadn't done so. To his knowledge, the dean was not an overtly religious man, nor did the conversation go further into the matter. But the question, from such an unexpected source, made an impact. Here he was, a person of faith, being encouraged by someone with a high position at an entirely secular institution!

By listening and observing without preconceptions, the dean had clarified his own identity—not as a religious person but as someone who had a common mission, a common cause, namely the student's success. Through that brief personal interaction, he made clear his stake in the outcome.

* * * *

To exemplify clarity of mission, one must embrace a ***lighthouse leadership*** approach. This aptly describes the leadership characteristics of Nelson Mandela or New Zealand prime minister Jacinda Ardern. They provided *a clear, visible point of reference* for others facing challenging and difficult times. Eventually, the "light" they provided led others to adopt the same mission as their own.

To be such a leader requires resilience—as exemplified by actual lighthouse structures in storm conditions. It also requires clarity, openness, and transparency. Like a literal lighthouse, a true leader cannot hide behind jargon or procedural technique.

The whole point is to be seen as a stable reminder of where the hazards lie, and what is the best course of action. A leader's values must be visible, as a guide for others seeking to follow the same.

The lighthouse metaphor has another useful application. A literal lighthouse does not *compel* ships to steer away from danger and toward safe harbor, even though it clearly marks the way there. It marks the way, but it does not make others' decisions for them. This is the same for a lighthouse leader. By providing a clear path through difficulties, he is not a typical, transactional boss. He can demonstrate, enlighten, and encourage but does not try to offer perks or threaten dire consequences to force compliance. By being a visible source of guidance and experience, he will help his teams navigate, as it were, and maintain focus on their shared long-term objectives.

As you contemplate what it means to lead "outside the boss," always remember that *the ends do not justify the means*. You may have a clear idea in your own mind of where you want to go—what you want your company or organization to achieve. But if you use a transactional, carrot-and-stick approach, you'll not only be of disservice to your people; you will also undermine your own success. Even if the perceived end is a noble one, the "I'm-the-boss" approach diminishes those who work for you, reducing them to mere commodities or "human resources" to be controlled. Once they realize that the boss disregards their vision, considers it irrelevant, then the paycheck is the only reason to stay. They will see no value in anything else.

THE ENDS DO NOT JUSTIFY THE MEANS; THE MEANS DEFINE THE END—A MISSION THAT EVERYONE WILL SUPPORT.

The opposite is true for a leader who understands clarity of mission: *the means **define** the end*. If the means and methods a leader uses are *people-centric*, empowering them to serve a common mission, then the result is anything but cold and transactional. This means prioritizing teamwork, recognizing people's accomplishments, investing in their skills, and connecting them with opportunities to learn and advance their positions. It also means giving them autonomy and the opportunity to problem-solve on their own—instead of endlessly micromanaging them. When these are the means you employ, the end will be a mission that everyone will support wholeheartedly.

This requires courage, work, and commitment because it goes against common dysfunctional practices. It is especially difficult when there's a backlog of transactional boss behavior and mistrust to overcome. Leading by example, an "outside the boss" approach gives a leader the power to accomplish greatness, both individually and collectively.

When a leader attempts to impart a true clarity of mission, he must do so with the knowledge that he'll be misunderstood—and often resisted by those he's trying to lead. He may understand clearly the company's "common denominator"—something that will combine the needs and goals of his people with those of his organization. However, it will often challenge people's assumptions, as it did for Alcoa's one-time CEO, Paul O'Neill.

GOOD CULTURE IS PROFITABLE

For over a century, Alcoa has been one of the world's largest aluminum producers, but in 1987, the company was in trouble. Poor financial performance, international competition, and market volatility, coupled with severe safety-related labor disputes had investors worried and public confidence at an all-time low.* The time was right for a change in leadership, but the new leader was anything but typical.

O'Neill had been in government service for sixteen years before entering the private sector. He had served as International Paper's president for only two years before his debut at Alcoa. To put it mildly, he was an unlikely choice. At the first official meeting, curious (and nervous) stockholders attended in greater numbers than usual to hear how O'Neill planned to change Alcoa's fortunes. To their dismay and confusion, he began the now-famous meeting with the words, "I want to talk to you about worker safety."

O'Neill went on to describe the company's hazardous plant conditions, where people worked with metals at 1,500 degrees and with machines that could rip off an arm. Even though the company's safety record wasn't the worst in the industry, he

---

*In 1986, a multistate strike involving 15,000 workers was only the latest in a long line of contentious labor disputes, which had peaked during World War II.

kept talking about it, and about his goal to achieve "zero injuries." He rebuffed audience questions on profitability, capital ratios, market opportunities, or any of the typical CEO talking points. Audience members were dumbfounded, wondering if their leader had gone mad, with many planning to sell their stock.

But shortly after O'Neill's bombshell, Alcoa's trajectory changed dramatically. As workers realized how serious he was about safety, they became personally engaged, not only about safe working conditions but also about the company's industrial process as a whole. They resonated emotionally with the idea of working in a safer environment—a mission and purpose that coincided with their CEO's overall mission of improving every aspect of Alcoa's process.[3]

O'Neill did not confine his mission to words. Following a fatal incident that happened only months after he took the helm, he convened a meeting of the plant's executives to remind them that the death was a failure of the entire chain of command. They went through every detail of the incident, absolving no one of responsibility and implementing unprecedented changes. After subsequent tragic events, his response was the same. Workers and managers alike saw that the company culture of accepting accidents as a cost of doing business would have to change permanently.

In the end, O'Neill's shared mission, and his determination to lead by example, produced remarkable results. During his tenure, Alcoa's market value increased from three billion to over twenty-seven billion dollars, and the company's safety record is one of the best in the world.

Paul O'Neill knew that if he actually *cared* about his employees' well-being—by doing something, not just mouthing platitudes—they would start seeing the bigger picture. His is not the only example of leading by example, of course.

- Starbucks CEO Howard Schultz implemented health-care coverage for part-time workers and introduced tuition assistance programs for employees.

- Southwest Airlines cofounder and CEO Herb Kelleher created a remarkable workplace culture that actively supported its employees, empowering them to make decisions and solve problems.[4]

- Marriott International chairman and CEO Bill Marriott often said that the four most important words in business were "What do you think?" The hotel giant's phenomenal success is credited to his emphasis on putting employees first.[5]

- Besides her leadership in the shift to electric vehicles, GM CEO Mary Barra has become known for her focus on employees' concerns and ideas, and her willingness to take responsibility for failures.[6]

None of these leaders is a perfect example, nor is there a

guarantee that an entire company, especially one that is large and complex, will continue to thrive. But experience shows that those companies—large and small—whose shared mission is clear will succeed where boss-driven, hierarchical companies cannot.

The Why and the How

When considering such an unconventional mission, it's only natural to ask why. Having shared clarity of mission is not easy. Human beings can be a stubborn lot. It can take time—sometimes lots of it—to get beyond your people's bad past experiences or their cultural biases. Also, a true mission doesn't have a definitive endpoint, a time where you can say, "Finally, we've reached our goal. Our business is everything we imagined it could be." After you've built a certain amount of trust and good communication, you'll see progress, but there's always something around the next corner.

> ## AN ENGAGED WORKFORCE AND A HUMAN-CENTERED COMPANY CULTURE WILL RESULT IN A SUCCESSFUL BUSINESS.

The most obvious reason to do this is of course the success of your business—the core of your mission. But the reasons go beyond business success. In chapter 10, we looked at mission as having three layers of meaning and purpose (see page 132), the first one being what goes on within the organization. As we've seen, an engaged workforce creates a successful company, but what happens outside the company? At the next level, the customers' experience with that mission is nothing but positive. They are more likely to remain customers, to the company's financial benefit, and to become *better* customers overall.

But perhaps the best reason why we do this occurs at the outermost layer, where the company's mission coincides with that of its people, their families, communities, and beyond. You may never know all the lasting effects of "paying it forward," but you can absolutely know what it does for your people. They are already engaged as employees, which advances your business, but they are also more likely to succeed beyond that—becoming great leaders themselves.

In my own business, as I complete the process of divesting, I can clearly see how others who shared in the mission are on track to succeed themselves.

* * * *

The ***how*** aspect of creating clarity of mission has many moving parts, but all of these begin with the leader's vision of who she truly is as a human being. True leadership is not about the mechanics; it's not simply a role to play or a set of procedures to follow. It's about the people you lead, knowing they can be trusted to carry their part of the mission because they trust you have their best interest as a top priority.

A true leader is the *initiator* of a culture of trust, a culture that begins and ends with communication and, above all, the absolute knowledge that the leader is human, not an infallible boss-god. That creates a collective ***kinetic energy*** that permeates the organization, creating a domino effect of greater and deeper engagement. The leader is the switch that keeps the energy flowing, but it is the people, each one vested in the mission, that drive that mission forward.

This isn't always obvious or acceptable to businessmen and entrepreneurs who are passionate about every aspect of their business. Some find it difficult to let go, thinking that things will fail if they're not involved in every detail. But in reality, trying to make everything happen by force of will has the opposite effect.

When each person in the organization "owns" his part of the mission, two things happen. First, everyone can sense almost immediately when things go right or wrong. Like the systems in the human body, everything is interconnected; a single failure at one point affects not only that part but every other part of the whole. The mission of the individual employee, both personal and professional, affects that of the entire company, and vice versa.

The second thing that happens is that the leader can release his people to do even greater things, knowing they will keep that kinetic energy flowing. By being the type of leader who initiates vulnerability, communication, and trust, he is ever more likely to receive it in return.

It Does Take a Village

Seeing around the next corner may work for an individual motorcycle or race-car driver, but in the real world, it's not a solo practice. It requires the participation of everyone with skills, intuition, and vision. This means every member of the organization, no matter what their role or how "ordinary" their tasks may be. Their skills and intuition may not be fully recognized or developed—or at least not yet. But to see what's around the corner, each member of an organization must have the same vision and purpose.

The legend of Atlas is instructive here. Many would-be bosses envision themselves as "holding up the heavens" through their unique and powerful attributes.* The reality is that their position of power is the result of his effort and the collective effort of all those involved in making success a reality. When leaders acknowledge and work hand in hand with employees as partners, their success is undoubtedly greater and more long-lived.

> ## SEEING AHEAD INVOLVES ACHIEVING A PURPOSE WHERE EVERYONE FEELS VESTED WITH EQUAL ENTHUSIASM.

Seeing ahead involves much more than one person "holding up the heavens." It means moving forward, not merely keeping the *status quo*. It involves achieving a purpose that everyone can envision and participate in with equal enthusiasm. It is in fact a partnership, a journey that requires everyone's contribution and insights in order to reach the goal.

Such a vision is not a solo journey; it requires the leader to do everything in his power to invite others to have a seat at the table—sharing their skills and talents to achieve the goals they have in common. The results, the impact and progress they make, must be something they can all see clearly. In effect, they will have become the ambassadors of the same mission and purpose, one that benefits them both, individually and collectively.

---

*For the record, the mythical Atlas's unending task was imposed as a punishment for defying the gods, not as an affirmation of his powers.

CHAPTER 12
MAKING THE MISSION COUNT

If you want to build a ship, don't drum up the men to gather wood, divide the work, and give orders. Instead, teach them to yearn for the vast and endless sea.

—ANTOINE DE SAINT-EXUPÉRY

Few other companies are better examples of clarity of mission than Patagonia, the outdoor clothing retailer and manufacturer founded in 1973. Presently organized as a private, for-profit "benefit corporation," the company is widely known for its support of social and environmental values. Although profitable, it has balanced company growth and value with responsibility for the planet.[1] In 2022, company founder Yvon Chouinard transferred ownership of the company to two separate trusts, ensuring that Patagonia's profits will continue to fight climate change.[2]

The company is also known for giving their employees a degree of autonomy or "agency," allowing them to take ownership and have input into the decisions that affect their work. In general, employees are made fully aware of the company's mission and shared values and are able to voice their opinions without fear of retaliation.

Pursuing this mission for five decades has not been an easy matter. In recent years, its values have been challenged by charges of poor labor conditions in its overseas manufacturing operations. In one instance (in 2011) it was found to be using a health-hazardous chemical. But its leaders have typically taken responsibility for shortcomings and contradictions, displaying an uncommon level of competent humility and vulnerability.[3]

Not all companies can embrace the same mission or cause, but all can have a mission that can be shared openly and clearly—one that includes the goals and aspirations of its people, and potentially beyond. So, in concluding this final piece of the leadership puzzle, we need to ask ourselves questions about our company's mission and about our capacity to make it clear to everyone.

QUESTIONS ABOUT CLARITY OF MISSION

Ask yourself the following questions, and take time to consider the answers you would have given years ago, in your leadership position right now, and in the not-so-distant future:

- Does your company or organization have a simple, easy-to-understand summary of its goals and aspirations? Was it created for marketing purposes, or something else? (How many of your people have actually read it and understand it?)

- To what extent does your company's mission emphasize efficiency, profitability, or competitive advantage?[*]

- To what extent does your mission reflect primarily the thinking and desires of you and your management team or other senior decision-makers?

- How much time do you spend understanding the goals and aspirations of your employees?

- To what extent are your employees' goals and aspirations aligned with those of your company? Would they agree—or even be willing to discuss it?

- To what extent have your actions made your company mission clear? How do you know?

Clarity of mission, like the other aspects great leadership, cannot be objectively or scientifically measured. However, if you answer the questions truthfully, and take time to think about it, you'll know how clear your mission is in *your* mind and, more importantly, whether it's clear to everyone else.

For our last two role-playing scenarios, we'll imagine two types of entities who are well known for being focused on mission: startup companies and nonprofit organizations. Each of these tend to give their mission almost spiritual significance. For that reason, both types of organizations tend to start strong, with passionate, highly motivated members working long hours and

---

*NOTE: These are not bad things, so long as they do not take priority over the important things in your mission.

sparing no energy in pursuit of their objective. But, as with all human endeavors, an overt mission emphasis is not without problems. Undue pride and possessiveness, lack of open communication, and mistrust can easily derail an idealistic mission—and the company or nonprofit that first espoused it.

All Work and No "We"

The idea of shared working space is certainly not new. Artisans and workers of all kinds have often economized by seeking common locations and facilities that they could not afford on their own. That concept was applied with a vengeance in 2010, with the formation of WeWork, a "new" approach to finding shared, more flexible and collaborative office space for businesses and individuals in large cities.

The concept of attractive, flexible workspaces with shared amenities like cafes was attractive to other startups and solo entrepreneurs. The cost and inconvenience of traditional office space in large cities were a burden, one that WeWork promised to alleviate on a massive scale. Investors were excited; by 2019, the company was valued at forty-five billion dollars. But by 2023, its stock fell by more than 98 percent, leading to its bankruptcy filing that year.

There are many reasons for the company's demise, not the least of which was the quasi-messianic persona of its outspoken founder, Adam Neumann.[4] In his flamboyant pitches to investors, he alluded to his plans to go beyond commercial real estate (the original business model) and encompass "all aspects of people's lives, in both physical and digital worlds." Eventually, investors like SoftBank tired of the rhetoric—and of Neumann's ability to spend their money without discernable results—and the love affair ended with a crash.

Of course, there is nothing inherently wrong with having an aspirational mission. But Neumann's chaotic, often erratic "party-going" management style and his aggressive, demanding treatment of employees undermined an already overhyped mission and ultimately led to its failure.

So, as a hypothetical exercise, imagine yourself as head of a startup with a truly revolutionary idea—something that will change the way people work. (If you wish, you can make it about artificial intelligence, as you did in chapter 3.) With the cautionary tale of WeWork in mind, consider how you might impart a true sense of mission and vision. Consider the following:

· WeWork's avowed mission was considered the brainchild of a few individuals, including Neumann. Does your big idea originate with you, for the most part, or do you owe credit to the work of others? How do you express that? How do you treat others who have similar or contrary ideas?

· Let's suppose your big idea sounds simple but requires some sophisticated or specialized expertise to carry it out. How do you communicate both the basic concept and its more nuanced aspects?

· Startups typically require long hours by a relatively small group of people. How do you communicate the importance of their work—not only to the company and its founders/stockholders but also to them personally.

· If a member of the startup is seemingly better at something other than his current role, what do you do?

· When an aspect of the business fails to perform as

planned, do you take any responsibility? Do you participate in finding a solution to the problem?

· When you ask your employees to fulfill an aspect of the mission, are you willing to step in when needed? How do your employees know whether to trust you or not?

As with all previous hypotheticals, there are many ways that "thinking outside the boss" are interrelated. Here too, a clear, shared sense of mission is dependent on a leader's ability to be vulnerable, to communicate clearly and fairly, and to earn others' trust. With startups, as with any other endeavor, a true mission is one that is mutually beneficial.

Smart Code

Nonprofit organizations exist for an incredibly wide variety of purposes and causes, from alleviating hunger or homelessness to providing opportunities to underserved or disadvantaged groups. One such group, Girls Who Code, was founded in 2012 to increase opportunities for female participation in computer science classrooms—a traditionally male-dominated field. With contributions and sponsorships from major tech companies, the group has programs in all fifty states and in Canada, India, and the United Kingdom.

Overall, Girls Who Code has earned high ratings as one of the best nonprofits to work for.[5] For part-time employees in particular, the organization's mission and practices are well-aligned, with opportunities to engage and improve one's skills in a traditionally difficult environment.

For your final hypothetical example, think of a cause or goal that you'd like to see supported by a nonprofit group or charity.

Put yourself in the shoes of a nonprofit founder like Reshma Saujani, the one-time politician who started Girls Who Code, and consider the following:

- Nonprofits perennially find funding a challenge. When presenting your case to potential supporters, how do you describe the origins of your group's mission? Is it primarily your big idea, or were others involved?

- Nonprofit operations often involve complex dealings with governments and other bureaucratic entities. Errors and gaps in knowledge are all too common. When these occur, do you take responsibility? Can you admit when you don't know something?

- Positions within nonprofits are often filled by volunteers or employees at relatively low pay rates. Other than their affinity for the group's goals, how do you communicate the group's mission as a benefit to them?

- A mission like that of Girls Who Code can lead to other aspirational goals, like equitable hiring practices. How do you keep your nonprofit's mission from expanding beyond your current capacity?

- No nonprofit has a perfect record of achievement. When your group's actions fall short of its mission objectives, how do you communicate that—and to whom?

Clarity of mission is a positive for every organization, no matter how noble or how ordinary that mission may be. By making that mission coincide with that of your people, and by ensuring that your actions can be trusted, you create a powerful and enduring leadership legacy.

THINKING OUTSIDE THE BOSS

We live in extraordinarily difficult times. Everywhere we look, the hierarchical, "I'm-the-boss-so-do-what-I-say" way of doing things has affected—one might say *infected*—institutions large and small, public and private. It affects us personally. Whether we are leading organizations or working in them, our sense of purpose, goals, and aspirations are frustrated on a daily basis.

The traditional carrot-and-stick leadership model is clearly broken. There are those who say it has never worked. To be sure, pyramids and palaces and profits have come from different versions of the "I'm the boss" model, but these have come at an enormous price. Ultimately, the transactional leadership model is doomed to failure.

> # IF YOU WANT TO BUILD A BUSINESS OR A CAUSE, ALWAYS START BY BUILDING UP YOUR PEOPLE.

There is a far better, more fundamental way. If you want to build a business or a cause, you must start by building up your people first. When you take the time to *listen*, and to facilitate your people operating in their strengths, they bring their best game to the match. They bring forward their creative strengths— even some they barely knew they had. They do it not because of perks or paychecks, not by wielding carrots or sticks, but because doing so satisfies the deepest human desire to belong and to have meaning.

* * * *

I am challenged regularly by business leaders who have convinced themselves that these ideas are a pipe dream. One particular skeptic is constantly challenging the whole idea of vulnerability, communication, trust, and mutual clarity of mission. "It can never work in the real world," he insists while in the midst of putting out fires on a daily basis as a result of a dysfunctional I'm-the-boss-do-what-I-say culture. My only answer is "Look at the results." I have been running successful businesses for three decades based solely on these principles. Others have achieved comparable results. It is not about good feelings or political correctness. As Paul O'Neill and so many other great leaders have proved, **good culture is not just a feel-good concept; it is actually profitable.** If you build great people, you'll have a great business.

When people operate from their strengths and talents, others see their best side, the "better angels" they were meant to be. The job of a leader is to look for those strengths, reflect them back to the person who has them, to show them what you see. Then help them smooth out the rough places, strengthen the weak parts, and become a better version of who they are. The more you do this, the more successful your business will be.

But everything starts with you becoming a better you, not by being a better boss. When you know you're not a superhero or a monarch, when you communicate and cultivate trust, and when your mission and others' are clear and mutual, success will surely follow. You'll be thinking outside the boss.

ENDNOTES

INTRODUCTION

1   Michael Gonchar, "What Objects Tell the Story of Your Life?" *New York Times*, September 30, 2014, https://archive.nytimes.com/learning. blogs.nytimes.com/2014/09/30/what-objects-tell-the-story-of-your-life/.

2   Paul Goldberger, "Buildings Speak to Us—How to Listen," *New York Times*, April 25, 1976. https://www.nytimes.com/1976/04/25/archives/buildings-speak-to-us-how-to-listen-buildings-speak-to-us-heres-how. html.

CHAPTER 1: OPENING THE DOOR

1   Bradley P. Owens et al., "The Impact of Leader Moral Humility on Follower Moral Self-Efficacy and Behavior," *Journal of Applied Psychology* 104, no. 1 (January 2019): 146–63, https://doi.org/10.1037/apl0000353.

2   Bradley P. Owens and David R. Hekman, "How Does Leader Humility Influence Team Performance? Exploring the Mechanisms of Contagion and Collective Promotion Focus," *Academy of Management Journal* 59, no. 3 (June 2016): 1088–1111, https://doi.org/10.5465/amj.2013.0660.

3   Mark Murphy, "3 Tests for Toxic Positivity in Your Organization," *Forbes*, September 29, 2023, https://www.forbes.com/sites/markmurphy/2023/09/28/three-tests-for-toxic-positivity-in-your-organization/.

4   Yonason Goldson, "Stop Trying to Find Fault in Others," *FastCompany*, April 30, 2023, https://www.fastcompany.com/90888558/this-is-what-happens-when-you-stop-looking-for-faults-in-others.

5   Caitlin Duffy and Jordan Turner, "Employees Seek Personal Value and

Purpose at Work. Be Prepared to Deliver," *Gartner*, March 29, 2023, https://www.gartner.com/en/articles/employees-seek-personal-value-and-purpose-at-work-be-prepared-to-deliver.

6   Shannon Schuyler, "Putting Purpose to Work: A study of Purpose in the Workplace ," *PwC*, June 2016, https://www.pwc.com/us/en/purpose-workplace-study.html.

CHAPTER 2: VULNERABILITY IS NOT WEAKNESS

1   Bill Eddy, "Are Narcissists and Sociopaths Increasing?" *Psychology Today*, April 30, 2018, https://www.psychologytoday.com/us/blog/5-types-people-who-can-ruin-your-life/201804/are-narcissists-and-sociopaths-increasing.

2   Jack McDonough, "He Tried to Avert the Challenger Disaster," *UMass Lowell*, January 1, 2021, https://www.uml.edu/engineering/research/engineering-solutions/roger-boisjoly-challenger.aspx.

3   Hugh Harris, "NASA, the *Challenger* Disaster, and How One Phone Call Could Have Saved the Crew," *Portalist*, January 28, 2019, https://theportalist.com/nasa-the-challenger-disaster-and-how-one-phone-call-could-have-saved-the-crew.

4   Daniel Kahneman, *Thinking, Fast and Slow* (New York: Farrar, Straus and Giroux, 2013).

5   "What Is a Key Performance Indicator (KPI)?" *Airfocus*, Accessed February 7, 2024, https://airfocus.com/glossary/what-is-a-key-performance-indicator/.

6   Josh Kaufman, *The Personal MBA: Master the Art of Business* (New York: Portfolio/Penguin, 2020).

CHAPTER 3: LEADERSHIP IN THE OPEN

1   "Gartner Hype Cycle," *Gartner Group*, https://www.gartner.com/en/research/methodologies/gartner-hype-cycle.

2   "Artificial Intelligence: Last Week Tonight with John Oliver (HBO)," *YouTube*, February 27, 2023, https://www.youtube.com/watch?v=Sqa8Z02XWc4.

3   Darren Woolley, "Which Half of My Advertising Is Wasted—and Is It Only Half?" *MediaVillage*, September 4, 2019, https://www.mediavillage.com/article/which-half-of-my-advertising-is-wasted-and-it-is-only-half/.

4   Rex Briggs and Greg Stuart, *What Sticks: Why Most Advertising Fails and How to Guarantee Yours Succeeds* (Chicago: Kaplan Publishing, 2006).

CHAPTER 4: MIXED SIGNALS

1   Dave Lee, "Nokia: The Rise and Fall of a Mobile Giant," *BBC News*, September 3, 2013, https://www.bbc.com/news/technology-23947212.

2   Songhe Wang, "Explanations to the Failure of Nokia Phone," *Proceedings of the 2022 7th International Conference on Financial Innovation and Economic Development (ICFIED 2022)*, March 26, 2022, https://doi.org/10.2991/aebmr.k.220307.307.

3   Charles Gaudet, "Where Did Nokia Go Wrong? (and Six Lessons You Can Learn from Them)," *Predictable Profits*, December 19, 2023, https://predictableprofits.com/where-did-nokia-go-wrong-and-six-lessons-you-can-learn-from-them/.

4   Rod Hise, "What Led to Nokia's Fall? Bad Communication," *InBusiness*, October 11, 2018, https://www.ibmadison.com/viewpoints/open-mic/what-led-to-nokias-fall-bad-communication/article_42a33cb9-2a8b-5690-9a2e-087cebba133e.html.

5   Anne C. Mulkern, "BP's PR Blunders Mirror Exxon's, Appear Destined for Record Book," *New York Times*, June 10, 2010, https://archive.nytimes.com/www.nytimes.com/gwire/2010/06/10/10greenwire-bps-pr-blunders-mirror-exxons-appear-destined-98819.html.

6   "US Oil Spill: 'Bad Management' Led to BP Disaster," *BBC News*, January 6, 2011, https://www.bbc.com/news/world-us-canada-12124830.

7   Morgan Galbraith, "Don't Just Tell Employees Organizational Changes Are Coming—Explain Why," *Harvard Business Review, October 5, 2018,* https://hbr.org/2018/10/dont-just-tell-employees-organizational-changes-are-coming-explain-why.

8   Jason Ballard, "Mastering The Art Of Effective Communication: Building Productivity And Collaboration," *Forbes*, May 20, 2024, https://www.forbes.com/councils/forbescoachescouncil/2024/05/20/mastering-the-art-of-effective-communication-building-productivity-and-collaboration/.

9   John Baldoni, "New Study: How Communication Drives Performance," *Harvard Business Review*, August 30, 2021, https://hbr.org/2009/11/new-study-how-communication-dr.

10   Alain Hunkins, "The #1 Obstacle to Effective Communication," *Forbes*, Sep 15, 2022, https://www.forbes.com/sites/alainhunkins/2022/09/15/the-1-obstacle-to-effective-communication/.

11   Jim Milliot, "Tracking 20 Years of Bookstore Chains," *Publishers Weekly*, August 26, 2011, https://www.publishersweekly.com/pw/by-topic/industry-news/bookselling/article/48473-tracking-20-years-of-bookstore-chains.html.

12   Elizabeth A. Harris, "How Barnes & Noble Went from Villain to Hero,"

New York Times, April 15, 2022, https://www.nytimes.com/2022/04/15/arts/barnes-noble-bookstores.html.

13   Stephen Wunker, "Barnes & Noble's Smart Strategy," *Harvard Business Review*, June 29, 2011, https://hbr.org/2011/06/barnes-nobles-smart-strategy.

CHAPTER 5: LISTENING TO UNDERSTAND

1   Daniel H. Pink, *Drive: The Surprise Truth About What Motivates Us* (New York: Riverhead Books, 2009).

2   "Comunicación Horizontal: Decálogo Para Puestos Directivos," *Santander Open Academy* blog, June 6, 2022, https://www.santanderopenacademy.com/es/blog/comunicacion-horizontal.html.

3   "8.5 Communication Channels," Chapter in *Exploring Business*, University of Minnesota Libraries, 2010, https://open.lib.umn.edu/exploringbusiness/chapter/8-5-communication-channels/.

4   "Do's and Don'ts to Get Employee Surveys Right," *Sogolytics*, March 15, 2024, https://www.sogolytics.com/blog/get-employee-surveys-right/.

5   Kate Gibson, "5 Professional Development Opportunities You Should Consider When Advancing Your Career," *Business Insights* blog, Harvard Business School, May 9, 2023, https://online.hbs.edu/blog/post/professional-development-opportunities.

6   Kara Baskin, "To Keep Employees, Focus on Career Advancement," *MIT Sloan Management*, June 13, 2023, https://mitsloan.mit.edu/ideas-made-to-matter/to-keep-employees-focus-career-advancement.

7   Helen Tupper and Sarah Ellis, "4 Experiments to Encourage Employees' Career Progress," *Harvard Business Review*, March 22, 2024, https://hbr.org/2024/03/4-experiments-to-encourage-employees-career-progress.

8   Alycia Wolf, "How to Use Future Casting to Redesign the Future," *Strategy Group*, January 24, 2024, https://www.thestrategygroup.com.au/redesign-future-2/.

9   James Harter et al., "Business-Unit-Level Relationship between Employee Satisfaction, Employee Engagement, and Business Outcomes: A Meta-Analysis," *Journal of Applied Psychology* 87, no. 2 (2002): 268–79, https://doi.org/10.1037/0021-9010.87.2.268.

CHAPTER 6: KEEPING THE CONVERSATION FLOWING

1   Daniel B. Kline, "These Are the Companies Americans Like Least," *Motley Fool*, May 29, 2019, https://www.fool.com/investing/2019/05/29/

companies-americans-like-least-cable-survey.aspx.

2   Stephanie Braun, "The History of Retail: A Timeline," *Lightspeed*, May
     8, 2015, https://www.lightspeedhq.com/blog/the-history-of-retail-a-
     timeline/.

CHAPTER 7: TAKING A LEAP

1   Paul J. Zak, "The Neuroscience of Trust," *Harvard Business Review*,
     January–February 2017, https://hbr.org/2017/01/the-neuroscience-of-
     trust.

2   C. Sue Carter, "Oxytocin and Human Evolution," *Behavioral
     Pharmacology of Neuropeptides: Oxytocin* 35 (2017): 291–319, https://doi.
     org/10.1007/7854_2017_18.

3   Daniel Kahneman, *Thinking, Fast and Slow* (New York: Farrar, Straus
     and Giroux, 2013).

4   "Air Traffic by the Numbers," *Federal Aviation Administration*, Accessed
     May 9, 2024, https://www.faa.gov/air_traffic/by_the_numbers.

5   James L. Gattuso, "Air Travel: A Hundred Years of Safety," *Mackinac
     Center*, October 6, 2003, https://www.mackinac.org/V2003-30.

6   Dominic Gates, "Global Air Travel Last Year: 22 Million Jet Flights,
     Just One Fatal Accident," *Seattle Times*, September 1, 2022, https://
     www.seattletimes.com/business/boeing-aerospace/global-air-travel-
     last-year-22-million-jet-flights-just-one-fatal-accident/.

7   "Deaths by Transportation Mode," *National Safety Council: Injury Facts*,
     May 6, 2024, https://injuryfacts.nsc.org/home-and-community/safety-
     topics/deaths-by-transportation-mode/.

8   Peter Robison, "Former Boeing Engineers Say Relentless Cost-Cutting
     Sacrificed Safety," *Bloomberg*, May 9, 2019, https://www.bloomberg.
     com/news/features/2019-05-09/former-boeing-engineers-say-
     relentless-cost-cutting-sacrificed-safety.

9   Justin Klawans, "How Boeing Dropped the Ball on Air Safety," *The
     Week*, January 16, 2024, https://theweek.com/business/boeing-air-
     safety-accidents-reputation.

10   Lauren Irwin, "Most in New Poll Say Air Travel Safe Despite Recent
     Incidents," *The Hill*, February 9, 2024, https://thehill.com/policy/
     transportation/4458054-poll-air-travel-safe/.

11   Chesley B. Sullenberger and Jeffrey Zaslow, *Highest Duty: My Search for
     What Really Matters* (New York: William Morrow & Company, 2010).

12   Rich Buhler and Staff, "Who Packs Your Parachute?–Truth!" *Truth or
     Fiction?*, March 16, 2015, https://www.truthorfiction.com/parachute/.

CHAPTER 8: BUILDING BONDS THAT LAST

1   Paul Zak, *"The Neuroscience of Trust."*

2   Bob Chapman and Rajendra Sisodia, *Everybody Matters: The Extraordinary Power of Caring for Your People Like Family* (London: Portfolio Penguin, 2016).

3   Rachel Feintzeig, "Flexibility at Work: Worth Skipping a Raise?" *Wall Street Journal*, October 31, 2014, https://www.wsj.com/articles/BL-ATWORKB-2141.

4   Ana Burcharth et al., "The Role of Employee Autonomy for Open Innovation Performance," *Business Process Management Journal* 23, no. 6 (November 6, 2017): 1245–69, https://doi.org/10.1108/bpmj-10-2016-0209.

5   Rebecca Brauchli et al., "Job Autonomy Buffers the Impact of Work–Life Conflict on Organizational Outcomes," *Swiss Journal of Psychology* 73, no. 2 (January 2014), https://doi.org/10.1024/1421-0185/a000126.

6   Nikki Blacksmith and Jim Harter, "Majority of American Workers Not Engaged in Their Jobs," Gallup.com, Oct. 28, 2011, https://news.gallup.com/poll/150383/majority-american-workers-not-engaged-jobs.aspx.

7   Thomas Chamorro-Premuzic, "Does Money Really Affect Motivation?" *Harvard Business Review*, April 10, 2013, https://hbr.org/2013/04/does-money-really-affect-motiv.

8   Ashley Reichheld and Amelia Dunlop, "How to Build a High-Trust Workplace," *MIT Sloan Management Review*, January 24, 2023, https://sloanreview.mit.edu/article/how-to-build-a-high-trust-workplace/.

9   Amy Gallo, "Managing Yourself: What Is Active Listening?" *Harvard Business Review*, January 2, 2024, https://hbr.org/2024/01/what-is-active-listening.

10 Kim Mills, "Speaking of Psychology: Why Are People Drawn to Extreme Sports?" *American Psychological Association.* Accessed May 24, 2024, https://www.apa.org/news/podcasts/speaking-of-psychology/extreme-sports.

CHAPTER 9: HERE TO HELP

1   Diana B. Henriques, "Bernard Madoff, Architect of Largest Ponzi Scheme in History, Is Dead at 82," *New York Times*, April 14, 2021, https://www.nytimes.com/2021/04/14/business/bernie-madoff-dead.html.

2   David Yaffe-Bellany et al., "Sam Bankman-Fried Is Found Guilty of 7 Counts of Fraud and Conspiracy," *New York Times*, November 2, 2023,

https://www.nytimes.com/2023/11/02/technology/sam-bankman-fried-fraud-trial-ftx.html.

3   Brad M. Barber and Terrance Odean, "Trading Is Hazardous to Your Wealth: The Common Stock Investment Performance of Individual Investors," *SSRN Electronic Journal*, April 12, 2000, https://doi.org/10.2139/ssrn.219228.

4   Andrew Bloomenthal, "Warren Buffett's Investing Strategy: An Inside Look," *Investopedia*, December 26, 2022, https://www.investopedia.com/investing/warren-buffetts-investing-style-reviewed/.

5   "Election Insights: Understanding Public Preferences for News Coverage for 2024," *AP-NORC*, May 1, 2024, https://apnorc.org/projects/election-insights-understanding-public-preferences-for-news-coverage-for-2024/.

6   Jan Hubbard, "Jordan Had to Grow to Trust Teammates for Bulls to Become Great," *Baltimore Sun*, Updated October 25, 2018, https://www.baltimoresun.com/1991/06/11/jordan-had-to-grow-to-trust-teammates-for-bulls-to-become-great/.

CHAPTER 10: THE IMPORTANCE OF MISSION

1   Henry Mintzberg and James A. Waters, "Of Strategies, Deliberate and Emergent," *Strategic Management Journal* 6 (1985): 257-272, https://onlinelibrary.wiley.com/doi/10.1002/smj.4250060306.

2   Jeroen Kraaijenbrink, "Why Your Mission and Vision Statements Don't Work (and What to Do about It)," *Forbes*, Updated April 14, 2022, https://www.forbes.com/sites/jeroenkraaijenbrink/2021/04/13/why-your-mission-and-vision-statements-dont-work-and-what-to-do-about-it/.

3   "The Meaning of Mission Statements," *Economist*, October 23, 2021, https://www.economist.com/business/2021/10/23/the-meaning-of-mission-statements.

4   Matt Murphy, "What Happened Next to the Thai Cave Rescue Boys?" *BBC News*, February 15, 2023, https://www.bbc.com/news/world-asia-64648769.

5   Lydia Smith and Sarah Jarvis, "Is the Term 'Wellness' Problematic?" *Patient*, Updated December 18, 2021, https://patient.info/news-and-features/is-the-term-wellness-meaningless.

6   Pete Nemmers, "Types of Hazards," *National Association of Safety Professionals*, December 26, 2018, https://naspweb.com/blog/types-of-hazards/.

7   M.J. Grawitch, M. Gottschalk, and D.C. Munz, "The path to a healthy

workplace: A critical review linking healthy workplace practices, employee well-being, and organizational improvements," *Consulting Psychology Journal: Practice and Research* 58, no. 3 (2006): 129–147, https://doi.org/10.1037/1065-9293.58.3.129.

8 Tracy Brower, "No Support for Career Development? 5 Ways to Succeed Anyway," *Forbes*, February 18, 2024, https://www.forbes.com/sites/tracybrower/2024/02/18/no-support-for-career-development-5-ways-to-succeed-anyway/.

9 Naina Dhingra et al., "Help Your Employees Find Purpose—Or Watch Them Leave," *McKinsey & Company*, April 5, 2021, https://www.mckinsey.com/capabilities/people-and-organizational-performance/our-insights/help-your-employees-find-purpose-or-watch-them-leave.

CHAPTER 11: SEEING AROUND THE CORNER

1 Trever Cartwright, "Finding Strength in What Makes Us Feel Vulnerable as a Leader," *Forbes*, October 22, 2023, https://www.forbes.com/sites/trevercartwright/2023/10/22/three-steps-to-finding-strength-in-what-makes-us-feel-vulnerable-as-a-leader/.

2 Valerij Dermol and Nada Trunk Širca, "Communication, Company Mission, Organizational Values, and Company Performance," *Procedia—Social and Behavioral Sciences* 238 (2018): 542-551, https://doi.org/10.1016/j.sbspro.2018.04.034.

3 David Burkus, "How Paul O'Neill Fought for Safety at Alcoa," *David Burkus* blog, Updated March 6, 2024, https://davidburkus.com/2020/04/how-paul-oneill-fought-for-safety-at-alcoa/.

4 Abner Valenzuela, "Herb Kelleher: A Servant Leader Who Soared with Southwest Airlines," *LinkedIn*, October 12, 2023, https://www.linkedin.com/pulse/herb-kelleher-servant-leader-who-soared-southwest-abner-y-valenzuela-ydctc/.

5 Steve Forbes, "How Bill Marriott's Putting Employees First Transformed a Family Root Beer Stand Into $14b Hotel Giant," *Forbes*, December 15, 2020, https://www.forbes.com/sites/steveforbes/2014/01/08/how-bill-marriotts-putting-employees-first-transformed-a-family-root-beer-stand-into-14b-hotel-giant/.

6 "Mary Barra Leadership Style," *Financhill*, October 31, 2020, https://financhill.com/blog/investing/mary-barra-leadership-style.

CHAPTER 12: MAKING THE MISSION COUNT

1 Tony Hansen, "Patagonia Shows How Turning a Profit Doesn't Have to Cost the Earth," *McKinsey & Company*, April 20, 2023, https://www.

mckinsey.com/industries/agriculture/our-insights/patagonia-shows-how-turning-a-profit-doesnt-have-to-cost-the-earth.

2   "Yvon Chouinard: How A Reluctant Businessman Built the Patagonia Brand," *MarcomCentral*, January 18, 2024, https://marcom.com/yvon-chouinard-how-a-reluctant-businessman-built-the-patagonia-brand/.

3   Lauren Aratani, "We've lost the right to be 'pessimistic': Patagonia treads fine line tackling climate crisis as for-profit company," *Guardian*, March 12, 2023, https://www.theguardian.com/business/2023/mar/12/patagonia-climate-crisis-for-profit-company.

4   Matthew Zeitlin, "Why WeWork Went Wrong," *Guardian*, December 20, 2019, https://www.theguardian.com/business/2019/dec/20/why-wework-went-wrong.

5   "2023 Best Nonprofits to Work For," May 11, 2023, https://bestcompaniesgroup.com/best-nonprofits-to-work-for/winners/2023best-companies/.

ACKNOWLEDGMENTS

My deepest gratitude

to Eileen for your undying love and support and for being an amazing partner and mother to Samantha and Ashley,

to my mom, Isabel Pineda, for believing in me,

to Fernando and my amazing team that believed in our purpose and stood by my side through every challenge,

to my ImpactEleven family for their support, and

to the entire Amplify team for bringing this book to life.

ABOUT THE AUTHOR

Oskhar Pineda's unyielding dedication to the pillars of his employee-based foundational leadership has been the cornerstone of his more than three decades as a successful entrepreneur, CEO, venture capital investor, and keynote speaker.

Pineda is a team and community builder. His businesses have achieved consistent profitability and longevity through four economic recessions and unstable financial markets. Specializing in the construction and engineering industry, Pineda has led organizations by developing a culture of trust and quality for clients and providing an inspiring place for employees to have the opportunity to grow together, prioritizing mutual respect and excellence.

He has built long-term relationships with civil engineers, real estate conglomerates, and others to lead critical building-repair initiatives. As a thought leader, he now teaches and collaborates with organizations to be people-first, helping them build consistently cohesive teams, lasting foundational cultures, and the grit and compassion to develop robust, effective, and lifelong leadership.

in ▶ ◎ @OSKHARPINEDA